A Collection of West Texas Recipes

A Perfect Setting

The Junior League of Lubbock

A Perfect Setting

The Junior League of Lubbock

Published by The Junior League of Lubbock, Inc.
4205 84th Street
Lubbock, Texas 79423
(806) 794-8874

Library of Congress Catalog Number: 2005924114
ISBN: 0-9759478-0-X

Edited, Designed, and Manufactured by
Favorite Recipes® Press
An imprint of

FRP

P. O. Box 305142
Nashville, Tennessee 37230
800-358-0560

Art Director: Steve Newman
Book Design: Travis Rader
Project Editor: Linda Bennie

Manufactured in the United States of America
First Printing: 2005
12,500 copies

Proceeds benefit charitable projects in the Lubbock community.

Photography Credits

Foreword

My grandmother and my mother were great cooks in Lubbock. I use a lot less butter and lard than they did and make less fried food, but I learned a lot from them about keeping my family healthy and happy. Mother, Melba Tatom Maxey, was very skilled at seasoning, a talent that I inherited and

developed further. Even with a busy career as a painter and sculptor, I always made time to create good meals, in addition to my art. We didn't have the fancy gourmet kitchens you can find now in many Lubbock homes, but we made some great dishes anyway. Besides the countless art shows I entered, what my kids remember most about growing up are all the fun times we had in the kitchen and around the dinner table. They are continuing the tradition. My daughter, Jill, married Harry Connick, Jr., from New Orleans, and they spend hours in the kitchen concocting elaborate, wonderful food. My son, Tim, married Denise, of Italian descent, so, of course, cooking is important to them, despite very busy lives, too. Denise makes the best carrot cake I've ever had in my life. My sister Carla is renowned in Lubbock for her coconut cake (see page 199). The meal most requested of me is my simple but delicious pot roast (see page 14). I have even cooked it for Dick and Lynn Cheney when they happened to visit Santa Fe, and they loved it! Lubbock is a model community for continuing the traditions of family in the kitchen. I hope busy young parents today can resist the temptations of fast food and chain restaurants to continue these traditions and create wonderful meals and lasting memories for their families.

Glenna Goodacre

Introduction

Food speaks to us as a series of memories—memories that are funny and sad, tender and sweet.

Food speaks of people and places, of simpler times and long-forgotten memories of the past. We remember all those dinner tables where the day's events were discussed; where our futures were planned; where friends and kindred spirits gathered for the most grand holiday meal, as well as the most simple of snacks.

Food takes us back to our childhood and family reunions, with plates piled high. It reunites us with the warm, comforting aromas of our past. Food speaks to us of friendship, of love, of caring, and sharing, perhaps because there exists a special bond between friends and family who dine together—a bond that is created, nurtured, treasured, and remembered.

West Texas hospitality creates its own special bond between people— a bond that is as special and diverse as a wonderful West Texas sunrise or a magnificent sunset. West Texas hospitality extends itself to extraordinary lengths to make a guest feel at home. West Texas hospitality recognizes the eternal bond between food and fellowship.

Therefore, in the tradition of West Texas hospitality, the women of the Junior League of Lubbock, Texas, are pleased to welcome you to *A Perfect Setting*.

Table of Contents

A Taste of Lubbock

Regional Flair

Texas Tailgating

Photograph courtesy of Duward Campbell

To create a setting for a barbecue, use a cowboy hat for a vase, red towels for napkins, and bandanas as bibs. Drinks can be served in large mason jars, or canned drinks can be placed in a galvanized tub filled with ice.

Green Chile Chowder

1/4 to 1/2 cup jalapeño chiles,
    seeded and minced
1/4 cup frozen green chiles, thawed
    and chopped
1 cup finely chopped onion
3 or 4 potatoes, cut into
    1/2-inch pieces
2 garlic cloves, minced

4 cups chicken broth
1/2 teaspoon salt
1/3 cup margarine
1/3 cup all-purpose flour
3 cups milk
1 cup (4 ounces) shredded
    Cheddar cheese

Combine the jalapeño chiles, green chiles, onion, potatoes, garlic, chicken broth and salt in a stockpot over high heat. Bring to a boil. Reduce the heat and simmer for 20 minutes. Melt the margarine in a saucepan over low heat. Add the flour and cook for 3 minutes, whisking constantly. Drain the jalapeño chile mixture, reserving the jalapeño chile mixture and the liquid. Add the reserved liquid to the flour mixture. Cook over medium heat until thickened, whisking constantly. Add the milk and cook until thickened, stirring constantly. Remove from the heat. Add the reserved jalapeño chile mixture and mix well. Cook until heated through, stirring occasionally. Ladle into soup bowls. Sprinkle each serving with 2 tablespoons of the cheese. *Serves 8.*

Cilantro is a Spanish name for a parsley-like plant that is also known as coriander or Chinese parsley. It has a distinctive peppery aroma and is used in many spicy Mexican dishes.

Texas Caviar

2 cans black beans, drained
2 cans black-eyed peas, drained
2 cans Shoe Peg corn, drained
2 cans tomatoes with green chiles
1 bunch cilantro, chopped
1 green bell pepper, chopped
1 yellow bell pepper, chopped
1 red bell pepper, chopped

1 purple onion, chopped
1 or 2 jalapeño chiles,
    finely chopped
1/4 cup red wine vinegar
1/4 cup lime and chile vinegar
Salt and black pepper to taste
Cayenne pepper to taste
Chili powder to taste

Combine the black beans, black-eyed peas, Shoe Peg corn, tomatoes with green chiles, cilantro, green bell pepper, yellow bell pepper, red bell pepper, onion, jalapeño chiles, red wine vinegar, lime and chili vinegar, salt, black pepper, cayenne pepper and chili powder in a bowl and mix well. Chill, covered, for 8 to 10 hours; drain. Serve with corn chips or tortilla chips. *Serves 30.*

The Best Picante Sauce

2 jalapeño chiles
1 garlic clove
1/4 cup chopped onion
1 to 2 tablespoons salt
1/4 teaspoon garlic powder
1/4 teaspoon ground cumin
1/4 teaspoon cayenne pepper
1 teaspoon chili powder
1/4 teaspoon sweet basil
1 (32-ounce) can whole tomatoes
1/4 cup apple cider vinegar

Combine the jalapeño chiles, garlic and onion in a food processor and process until blended. Add the salt, garlic powder, cumin, cayenne pepper, chili powder, basil, tomatoes and vinegar and process until of the desired consistency. Pour into hot sterilized jars. Store, covered, in the refrigerator for up to 4 weeks. Serve with chips. ***Makes 3 pints.***

Spicy Pecans

1 pound pecan halves
2 tablespoons unsalted butter
1 1/2 teaspoon ground cumin
1/4 teaspoon cayenne pepper
2 tablespoons sugar
1 teaspoon salt

Place the pecans in a metal bowl. Melt the butter in a saucepan. Remove from the heat. Add the cumin and cayenne pepper and stir for 30 seconds. Pour over the pecans. Add the sugar and salt and stir to coat. Spread in a 10×15-inch baking pan. Bake at 300 degrees for 15 minutes or until toasted, stirring occasionally; do not overbake. Serve warm or at room temperature. You may prepare the pecans up to 4 days in advance. Store in an airtight container. ***Makes 3 cups.***

Shelled nuts and seeds produce more flavor when toasted. They can be toasted either in a sauté pan on the stove or in a shallow baking pan in the oven. On the stove, use medium-high heat and toss gently to prevent burning. In the oven, toast at about 375 degrees for 1 to 2 minutes for small seeds and 5 to 10 minutes for larger nuts. Use your sense of smell to test for doneness.

White Chocolate Trail Mix

10 ounces miniature pretzels
5 cups Crispix cereal
5 cups Multigrain Cheerios cereal
5 cups Golden Grahams cereal
1 cup mixed nuts
16 ounces crispy "M & M's" Chocolate Candies
12 ounces vanilla chips
3 tablespoons canola oil

Combine the pretzels, Crispix, Cheerios, Golden Grahams, nuts and "M & M's" in a bowl and mix well. Combine the vanilla chips and canola oil in a microwave-safe bowl. Microwave on Low until the vanilla chips are melted, stirring frequently; do not burn. Pour over the pretzel mixture and toss to coat. Spread on waxed paper and let stand until cool. Store in an airtight container. *Serves 80.*

Puppy Chow

2 cups (12 ounces) chocolate chips
1 cup peanut butter
1/2 cup (1 stick) margarine
1 package rice Chex cereal
1 (1-pound) package confectioners' sugar

Combine the chocolate chips, peanut butter and margarine in a saucepan. Cook until melted, stirring constantly. Remove from the heat. Place the cereal in a large bowl or pan. Add the chocolate chip mixture and stir to coat. Add the confectioners' sugar and shake to coat. Store in an airtight container. *Serves 16 to 20.*

Glenna's Pot Roast

1 (3- to 4-pound) good-quality chuck roast or arm roast
All-purpose flour for coating
Lawry's seasoned salt to taste
Pepper to taste
Vegetable oil
1 onion, cut into large wedges
2 cups beef bouillon
1 large bay leaf, cut into halves
2 cups (3-inch) celery sticks
6 to 8 carrots, cut into 3-inch pieces
8 to 10 small new red potatoes, scrubbed
3 tablespoons all-purpose flour
1 cup water

Coat the roast with flour and sprinkle with seasoned salt and pepper. Heat oil in a Dutch oven. Cook the roast in the oil until brown on 1 side. Turn over the roast. Add the onion and cook until the roast and onion are brown; the onion will add flavor to the gravy. Add the beef bouillon and bay leaf halves.

Bake, covered, at 350 degrees for 2 to 2^1/$_2$ hours, basting and turning every 45 minutes. Sprinkle the celery, carrots and potatoes with seasoned salt and pepper and place in the Dutch oven with the roast. Bake, covered, for 30 minutes or until the potatoes are tender. Baste with the drippings.

Remove the roast and vegetables to a serving plate, reserving the drippings in the Dutch oven. Combine 3 tablespoons flour and the water in a bowl and mix well. Add to the reserved drippings. Bring to a boil and boil until thickened, stirring constantly and adding additional beef bouillon if needed. Spoon ^{1}/$_2$ of the gravy over the roast and vegetables. Serve with the remaining gravy, fresh salsa or spicy chutney, a salad and bread. *Serves 6.*

Raider Barbecue Brisket

2 tablespoons liquid smoke
4 pounds lean beef brisket
1 tablespoon onion salt
1 tablespoon garlic salt
3 tablespoons brown sugar
1 cup ketchup
1/4 cup water
1/2 teaspoon celery salt
1 tablespoon liquid smoke
2 tablespoons Worcestershire sauce
3 tablespoons prepared mustard
2 tablespoons red wine vinegar
Salt and pepper to taste

Pour 2 tablespoons liquid smoke evenly over the beef. Rub with the onion salt and garlic salt. Wrap in foil and chill for 8 to 10 hours. Place the beef in a roasting pan. Bake, covered, at 300 degrees for 5 to 6 hours or until cooked through. Let stand until cool. Slice the beef and return to the roasting pan.

Combine the brown sugar, ketchup, water, celery salt, 1 tablespoon liquid smoke, Worcestershire sauce, prepared mustard, vinegar, salt and pepper in a saucepan. Bring to a boil, stirring constantly. Pour over the beef. Bake, covered, for 1 hour or until heated through. *Serves 8 to 10.*

Beef Kabobs

2 cups vegetable oil
1¹/2 cups soy sauce
1 cup lemon juice
¹/2 cup Worcestershire sauce
¹/2 cup prepared mustard
2 to 4 teaspoons cracked pepper
4 garlic cloves
3 pounds sirloin steak, cut into 1¹/2-inch cubes
1 package smoked sausage, cut into 1-inch pieces
10 thick slices bacon, cut into 1¹/2-inch pieces
Tomatoes
Small onions
Green bell peppers, cut into pieces
Red bell peppers, cut into pieces
Mushrooms
Hot cooked rice

Combine the oil, soy sauce, lemon juice, Worcestershire sauce, prepared mustard, pepper and garlic in a blender and process until well mixed. Reserve a small amount of the oil mixture to serve as a sauce. Combine the steak, sausage and bacon in a bowl. Pour half the remaining oil mixture over the steak mixture and stir to coat. Combine the tomatoes, small onions, green bell peppers, red bell peppers and mushrooms in a bowl. Pour the remaining oil mixture over the vegetable mixture and stir to coat. Marinate the steak mixture and the vegetable mixture, covered, in the refrigerator for 24 to 36 hours.

Thread the steak, sausage and bacon alternately onto skewers, reserving the marinade. Thread the vegetables alternately onto skewers, reserving the marinade. Broil or grill the beef kabobs and vegetable kabobs until the vegetables are cooked through, basting frequently with the reserved marinade. Remove the vegetable kabobs to a plate and continue grilling the beef kabobs until cooked through. Remove to a plate. Remove the skewers from the kabobs. Serve over rice on a serving platter. Serve with the reserved sauce. *Serves 8.*

Beef Chili

1 pound ground beef
1 onion, chopped
1 garlic clove, minced
2 tablespoons chili powder
1 tablespoon all-purpose flour
1 teaspoon salt
1/8 teaspoon cayenne pepper
1 teaspoon crushed red pepper flakes
1/2 teaspoon ground cumin
1/2 teaspoon sugar
1/2 cup water
1 (16-ounce) can stewed tomatoes
1 can ranch-style beans, drained

Brown the ground beef with the onion and garlic in a skillet, stirring until crumbly; drain. Add the chili powder, flour, salt, cayenne pepper, red pepper flakes, cumin, sugar, water and undrained tomatoes and mix well. Pour into a slow cooker. Cook on Low for 5 to 6 hours or until done to taste. Stir in the beans. *Serves 4 to 6.*

When serving chili to a crowd of people, set out sour cream, shredded cheese, diced avocado, onion, and cilantro as accompaniments. Round out the meal with hot bread or corn bread and a green salad.

Tips for tailgating:

★ *Prepare as much as possible ahead of time.*

★ *Arrive early.*

★ *Make sure you have plenty of water, paper towels, and other supplies needed.*

★ *Have people to help.*

★ *Bring plenty of ice, both for drinks and to keep foods chilled.*

★ *Clean up your area before you leave.*

Bourbon-Spiced Pork Tenderloins

2 (1-pound) pork tenderloins
1/4 cup bourbon
1/4 cup soy sauce
1/4 cup Dijon mustard
1/4 cup packed brown sugar
1/4 cup olive oil
1 1/2 teaspoons ground ginger
2 teaspoons Worcestershire sauce
4 garlic cloves, minced

Place the pork in a nonreactive dish. Combine the bourbon, soy sauce, Dijon mustard, brown sugar, olive oil, ginger, Worcestershire sauce and garlic in a blender or food processor and process until blended. Pour over the pork, turning to coat. Marinate, covered, in the refrigerator for 8 to 10 hours. Drain, reserving the marinade. Grill over high heat until seared on all sides; do not pierce the pork. Reduce the heat to medium. Grill for 25 minutes or until the pork is cooked through, basting frequently with the reserved marinade. Remove to a plate and cover with foil. Let stand for 10 minutes before slicing. ***Serves 8.***

Summer Spareribs

5 pounds boneless country-style
  pork spareribs
1/4 cup Worcestershire sauce
1 1/2 onions, chopped
1 cup packed brown sugar
1 cup ketchup
1/4 cup vinegar
2 teaspoons dry mustard
1 1/2 cups water
1/4 teaspoon salt
1 teaspoon pepper

Arrange the spareribs in a 9×13-inch baking dish. Combine the Worcestershire sauce, onions, brown sugar, ketchup, vinegar, dry mustard, water, salt and pepper in a bowl and mix well. Pour over the spareribs. Bake, covered, at 350 degrees for 2 1/2 hours or until cooked through. ***Serves 12.***

Tailgate Oven Sandwiches

Dijon mustard (optional)
Mayonnaise (optional)
2 (8-count) packages onion buns
1 pound deli ham, thinly sliced
1 pound deli turkey, thinly sliced
1 pound Swiss cheese, sliced

Spread Dijon mustard and mayonnaise over the cut sides of the buns.
Place 2 or 3 slices of ham or turkey and 1 slice of cheese on a bun half and
top with the remaining bun half. Wrap the sandwich in foil. Repeat the
procedure with the remaining buns, ham, turkey and cheese. Bake at
300 degrees for 20 minutes. Transport the sandwiches in a cooler lined
with newspaper. *Serves 16.*

Mesquite-Smoked Turkey

1 (8- to 10-pound) turkey
3 tablespoons butter or margarine
2 tablespoons meat rub (preferably Cavender's)

Arrange mesquite wood chips in a smoker. Preheat the smoker to
300 degrees and heat for 30 minutes. Remove and discard the packet from
the turkey cavity. Rinse the turkey. Coat with the butter and rub with the
meat rub. Smoke over indirect heat for 2 to $2^{1}/2$ hours. Wrap in heavy-duty
foil. Bake at 250 degrees in the oven for 2 hours. You may grill the turkey on
a gas grill instead. For a smoky flavor, soak the mesquite wood chips in water
and wrap them in foil. Poke holes in the foil and place on the coals while
grilling the turkey. *Serves 12.*

Beer Chicken

1/2 onion, chopped
3 garlic cloves, chopped
1/4 cup olive oil
3 carrots, chopped into large pieces
2 boneless skinless whole chicken breasts
1/2 cup soy sauce
2 bottles or cans beer
1/2 cup packed brown sugar
1 teaspoon pepper
Salt and pepper to taste
Hot cooked rice

Brown the onion and garlic in the olive oil in a stockpot. Add the carrots and cook for 2 to 3 minutes. Stir in the chicken. Add the soy sauce, beer, brown sugar and 1 teaspoon pepper and mix well. Bring to a boil. Reduce the heat and simmer, partially covered, for 45 minutes. Remove the chicken to a cutting board and shred using 2 forks. Return the chicken to the stockpot. Cook, uncovered, over medium heat for 15 minutes or until the sauce is thickened. Season with salt and pepper to taste. Serve over rice. ***Serves 4.***

Oven-Fried Chicken

1/2 cup shortening
1/2 cup all-purpose flour
1 teaspoon salt
Dash of pepper
1 (12-count) package chicken drumettes

Melt the shortening in a baking dish in a preheated 400-degree oven. Maintain the oven temperature. Combine the flour, salt and pepper in a sealable plastic bag and shake to mix. Add the chicken in batches of 3 or 4 and shake to coat. Arrange the chicken in the hot shortening. Bake for 15 minutes. Turn over the chicken and bake for 15 minutes longer or until cooked through and tender. You may use other chicken pieces and adjust the baking time as needed. ***Serves 12.***

Tex-Mex Chicken Spaghetti

1 pound Velveeta cheese, cubed
1 can tomatoes with green chiles
1 can condensed cream of chicken soup
1 can condensed cream of mushroom soup
4 boneless skinless chicken breasts, or 6 chicken tenderloins,
   cooked and cut into bite-size pieces
12 ounces spaghetti, cooked and drained

Microwave the cheese in a microwave-safe bowl for $2^1/2$ minutes or until melted. Stir in the undrained tomatoes with green chiles. Microwave for $2^1/2$ minutes. Combine the cream of chicken soup, cream of mushroom soup, cheese mixture, chicken and spaghetti in a bowl and mix well. Grease a 9×13-inch baking dish or spray with nonstick cooking spray. Spoon the chicken mixture into the prepared baking dish. Bake at 350 degrees for 30 minutes. You may substitute Mexican Velveeta for the Velveeta and hot tomatoes with green chiles for the tomatoes with green chiles. **Serves 8.**

Venison Roll-Ups

Venison, cut into strips and tenderized
Italian salad dressing
Bacon
Swiss cheese, cut into strips

Combine the venison and salad dressing in a bowl and stir to coat. Chill, covered, until ready to bake. Drain the venison, reserving the salad dressing. Place a slice of bacon and a strip of cheese on top of a strip of venison and roll to enclose, securing with a wooden pick. Repeat the procedure with the remaining venison, bacon and cheese. Arrange the roll-ups in an 8×8-inch baking pan. Pour the reserved salad dressing evenly over the roll-ups. Bake, covered, at 350 degrees for 25 minutes or until cooked through, turning once. **Makes variable servings.**

Portobello Mushroom Fajitas

16 ounces portobello mushrooms, cut into slices

1 large 1040 Texas onion, cut into wedges

2 zucchini, cut into slices

2 yellow squash, cut into slices

1 large green bell pepper, cut lengthwise into slices

1 bottle gourmet marinade (such as hot plum chipotle or
papaya lime serrano)

Whole wheat tortillas, warmed

Shredded Monterey Jack cheese

Chopped avocados

Toasted pine nuts

Combine the portobello mushrooms, onion, zucchini, yellow squash, bell pepper and marinade in a sealable plastic bag or plastic container with a lid. Chill for 8 to 10 hours. Drain the vegetables. Place in a skillet over medium-high heat and cook for 20 minutes or until the onion is cooked through, stirring frequently. Spoon the vegetables onto tortillas. Sprinkle with cheese, avocados and pine nuts and fold to enclose. Serve immediately. **Serves 6.**

New Mexico Red Chile Enchiladas

2 tablespoons minced garlic
2 tablespoons olive oil
$^1/4$ teaspoon oregano
$^1/4$ teaspoon ground cumin
2 tablespoons all-purpose flour
$^1/4$ cup New Mexico red chile powder
$^1/4$ teaspoon salt
$2^1/2$ cups water
12 corn tortillas
2 cups (8 ounces) shredded Monterey Jack cheese
$^1/2$ cup chopped fresh cilantro
$^1/2$ cup pine nuts, toasted

Sauté the garlic in the olive oil in a skillet over low heat for 1 to
2 minutes. Add the oregano, cumin, flour, chile powder and salt and whisk
until a smooth paste forms. Add the water gradually, whisking constantly.
Simmer for 15 to 20 minutes, stirring frequently to prevent scorching. Ladle
$^1/3$ of the mixture into a 9×11-inch baking dish. Layer with 6 tortillas, $^1/3$ of
the cheese, $^1/2$ of the cilantro and $^1/2$ of the pine nuts. Repeat the layers and
top with the remaining cheese. Bake at 350 degrees for 30 minutes. **Serves 6.**

*Tex-Mex is a blending of
hearty Texas and flavorful
Mexican cuisines. The
enchilada was originally made
in Mexico with cheeses and a
chile gravy or sauce. Texas,
with its plentiful supply of
beef, adapted its own version
of the enchilada to include
either beef or chicken.*

Tequila Corn

1/4 cup minced shallots
1 small red bell pepper,
   finely chopped
1 tablespoon minced garlic
1 tablespoon olive oil
2 cans niblet corn
2 tablespoons tequila

1 tablespoon fresh lime juice
Salt to taste
2 cups heavy cream
1/4 cup finely chopped
   fresh cilantro
12 cherry tomatoes,
   cut into quarters

Sauté the shallots, bell pepper and garlic in the olive oil in a skillet over medium heat until tender. Add the corn, tequila, lime juice and salt and mix well. Cook over medium-high heat for about 4 minutes, stirring frequently. Add the cream, cilantro and cherry tomatoes and cook just until heated through, stirring occasionally. **Serves 6.**

Coach's Favorite Jalapeño Corn Bread

1 cup buttermilk
1 cup yellow cornmeal
1 cup sifted all-purpose flour
3 tablespoons sugar
1 teaspoon salt
1 teaspoon baking powder
1/2 teaspoon baking soda

1 egg, beaten
1/4 cup shortening, melted
1 (16-ounce) can corn, drained
2 cups (8 ounces) shredded
   Cheddar cheese
3 jalapeño chiles, chopped

Combine the buttermilk, cornmeal and flour in a bowl and mix well. Add the sugar, salt, baking powder, baking soda, egg, shortening, corn, cheese and jalapeño chiles and mix well. Pour into a greased 9×13-inch baking pan. Bake at 375 degrees for 30 minutes. You may substitute a different type of cheese for the Cheddar. **Serves 15.**

Apple Crumb Pie

3 cups sliced peeled Granny Smith apples
2/3 cup sugar
1 teaspoon ground cinnamon
1 unbaked (9-inch) pie shell
1/2 cup all-purpose flour
1/2 cup rolled oats
1/4 cup chopped nuts
1/2 cup (1 stick) butter, softened

Combine the apples, sugar and cinnamon in a bowl and mix well. Pour into the pie shell. Combine the flour, oats, nuts and butter in a bowl and mix until crumbly. Sprinkle evenly over the filling. Bake at 350 degrees for 40 to 45 minutes or until brown. **Serves 8.**

Pecan Pie

3 eggs, lightly beaten
1/2 cup granulated sugar
1 tablespoon brown sugar
1/2 teaspoon salt
2 tablespoons butter, melted
1 teaspoon vanilla extract
3/4 cup dark corn syrup
2 cups pecans
1 (1-crust) pie pastry

Combine the eggs, granulated sugar, brown sugar, salt, butter, vanilla and corn syrup in a bowl and mix well. Stir in the pecans. Fit the pie pastry into a 9-inch pie plate. Pour the pecan mixture into the pie shell. Bake at 325 degrees for 50 to 60 minutes. **Serves 6 to 8.**

Although pecans are available year-round, their peak season is in the fall. Select pecans with kernels that do not rattle when shaken. Shelled pecans can be refrigerated in an airtight container for several months or frozen for up to one year.

Creamy Lime Pie

2¹/2 cups graham cracker crumbs
¹/2 cup sugar
¹/2 cup (1 stick) margarine, melted
16 ounces cream cheese, softened
³/4 cup fresh lime juice
1 can sweetened condensed milk
Grated zest of 1 lime
1 cup heavy whipping cream
2 tablespoons confectioners' sugar

Combine the graham cracker crumbs, sugar and margarine in a bowl and mix well. Press over the bottom and up the side of two 8-inch pie plates. Bake at 375 degrees for 8 to 10 minutes. Let stand until completely cool.

Beat the cream cheese in a mixing bowl until creamy and smooth. Add the lime juice and beat until blended. Mix in the sweetened condensed milk and lime zest. Pour equal portions of the mixture into the pie shells. Chill, covered, for 6 to 10 hours.

Beat the cream and confectioners' sugar in a mixing bowl until soft peaks form. Spread over the lime filling. Garnish with lime slices. You may prepare this dessert in a 9×13-inch baking dish instead of two 8-inch pie plates.
Serves 12.

Microwave Peanut Brittle

1 cup raw peanuts
1/8 teaspoon salt
1 cup sugar
1/2 cup corn syrup

1 teaspoon butter or margarine
1 teaspoon vanilla extract
1 teaspoon baking soda

Butter a 10×15-inch pan or spray with nonstick cooking spray. Combine the peanuts, salt, sugar and corn syrup in a microwave-safe bowl. Microwave, uncovered, on High for 4 minutes; stir. Microwave for 3 minutes. Add the butter and mix well. Microwave for 2 minutes. Add the vanilla and baking soda and stir until foamy. Pour immediately into the prepared pan, spreading until very thin. Let stand until completely cool. Break into pieces. This recipe works best with high-wattage microwaves. **Serves 10 to 12.**

Texas Pralines

3 cups sugar
1 cup buttermilk
1 teaspoon baking soda
Pinch of salt

2 tablespoons butter
1 teaspoon vanilla extract
2 to 3 cups pecans
Salt

Combine the sugar, buttermilk, baking soda and pinch of salt in a 4-quart saucepan. Cook over medium heat to 235 degrees on a candy thermometer, soft-ball stage, stirring constantly. Remove from the heat. Add the butter, vanilla and pecans and stir just until creamy, adding a small amount of milk if the mixture is too thick. Drop by spoonfuls onto waxed paper that has been generously sprinkled with salt. **Makes (about) 5 dozen pralines.**

Thirst Quenchers

Beverages

Sips and Dips

Photograph courtesy of Mary Kay Ragan

Almost everything that would be served at a cocktail party or during a pre-meal cocktail hour is intended to be eaten with the fingers. Some of these foods are often served at regular meals as well (although not often very formal ones). When they are, it is still permissible to use the fingers to eat them. This includes olives, pickles, nuts, and chips.

Prickly Pear Sangria

1 (750-milliliter) bottle zinfandel
1 (750-milliliter) bottle cabernet
   sauvignon
1/4 cup crème de cassis
1/2 cup amaretto
2 cups orange juice
1 (11-ounce) can pear nectar
1 (11-ounce) can apricot nectar
1 cup prickly pear purée
2 tablespoons vanilla extract
2 cinnamon sticks

Sugar to taste
1 apple, thickly sliced
1 orange, thickly sliced
2 lemons, thickly sliced
2 limes, thickly sliced
Club soda to taste
1 apple, thinly sliced
1 orange, thinly sliced
2 lemons, thinly sliced
2 limes, thinly sliced

Combine the zinfandel, cabernet sauvignon, crème de cassis, amaretto, orange juice, pear nectar, apricot nectar, prickly pear purée, vanilla, cinnamon sticks and sugar in a glass pitcher and mix well. Add the thick slices of apple, orange, lemons and limes. Chill, covered, for 24 hours or longer. Remove and discard the fruit. Add the club soda and thin slices of apple, orange, lemons and limes. Pour over ice in glasses. **Makes 5 quarts.**

The word sangria *is Spanish for* blood, *denoting the rich, red color of the drink. Sangria is made with red wine, fruit, fruit juices, and soda water. It is usually served cold over ice and makes a refreshing drink any time of year.*

Sunset Sangria

$^1/_2$ to 1 cup sugar
$^1/_2$ to 1 cup water
1 large can frozen orange juice concentrate
1 small can frozen limeade concentrate
Juice of 2 lemons
Juice of 2 limes
Juice of 1 orange
Dry red wine to taste

Combine the sugar and water in a small saucepan and cook until the sugar is dissolved, stirring constantly, to make a simple syrup. Prepare the orange juice and limeade in a 1-gallon pitcher using the package directions. Add the simple syrup, lemon juice, lime juice, orange juice and wine and mix well. Garnish with sliced fruit. Pour over ice in glasses. **Serves 10.**

Green Apple Martinis

2 cups sweet-and-sour mix
1¹/2 cups vodka
1¹/2 cups green apple pucker

Fill a 10-cup pitcher half full with ice cubes. Add the sweet-and-sour mix, vodka and green apple pucker and stir to mix. Strain into martini glasses. Garnish each glass with a thin slice of Granny Smith apple. **Serves 6.**

*For **Caramel Apple Martinis**, add one ounce of butterscotch schnapps to each glass.*

Bahama Delight

¹/2 ounce rum
¹/2 ounce coconut rum
¹/2 ounce grenadine
1 ounce orange juice
1 ounce pineapple juice
1 cup crushed ice

Combine the rum, coconut rum, grenadine, orange juice, pineapple juice and crushed ice in a blender and process until slushy. Pour into a glass and serve. **Serves 1.**

Border Buttermilk

1 (12-ounce) can frozen pink lemonade concentrate
8 ounces vodka or tequila

Combine the pink lemonade concentrate and vodka in a blender. Add enough ice to reach the fill line and process until smooth. Pour into glasses and serve. **Serves 8.**

Bellinis

1 (750-milliliter) bottle Champagne
2 (11-ounce) cans peach nectar
1/2 cup peach schnapps

Combine the Champagne, peach nectar and peach schnapps in a pitcher and stir to mix. Pour into a freezer-safe 9×13-inch pan. Freeze, covered, until firm. Remove from the freezer 15 minutes before serving. Spoon into glasses and serve. **Serves 6.**

Margaritas in a Minute

4 (12-ounce) cans frozen limeade concentrate
3 quarts water
3 cups tequila
3 cups Triple Sec
2 (2-liter) bottles lemon-lime soda, chilled

Combine the limeade concentrate, water, tequila and Triple Sec in a bowl and mix well. Divide the mixture among several sealable freezer bags. Freeze for 24 hours or longer. Combine equal portions of limeade mixture and lemon-lime soda in a punch bowl and stir until slushy, breaking up any large pieces. Garnish with lime slices. Serve immediately. **Makes 2¹/2 gallons.**

Frozen Watermelon Margaritas

4 cups watermelon chunks, seeded and frozen
¹/2 cup tequila
¹/4 cup Triple Sec
¹/3 cup fresh lime juice
1 lime, cut into 4 wedges

Place ³/4 of the watermelon in a blender. Add the tequila, Triple Sec and lime juice and process until smooth. Add the remaining watermelon and process until blended. Pour into glasses. Squeeze the juice of 1 lime wedge into each glass and garnish with the lime wedge. **Serves 4.**

Lubbock is one of the world's leading manufacturers of cottonseed products and is a major U.S. cotton market. Cotton markets handle more than one billion pounds of cotton per year and produce more than one and one-half billion pounds of cottonseed oil.

Watermelon Mojitos

1 cup fresh mint leaves
$1/2$ cup sugar
$1^1/2$ cups light rum
$1/2$ cup fresh lime juice
$1/2$ cup watermelon juice
6 cups club soda
6 cups crushed ice

Combine the mint and sugar in a medium bowl and mash with a wooden spoon until the mint is aromatic and the oils are released. Add the rum and lime juice and stir until the sugar is dissolved. Add the watermelon juice and stir to mix. Strain into a pitcher. Add the club soda and stir gently. Fill each of 6 glasses with 1 cup crushed ice. Pour the beverage over the ice. Garnish each serving with a lime wedge. **Serves 6.**

Brandy Alexander Punch

1 gallon vanilla ice cream
1 cup brandy
1 cup Godiva chocolate liqueur

Combine the ice cream, brandy and chocolate liqueur in a mixing bowl and beat until smooth. Pour into a freezer-safe container and freeze, covered, until serving time. **Makes $1^1/2$ gallons.**

Caroline's Milk Punch

1 cup sugar
1/2 cup water
1 fifth of bourbon
3 quarts milk
1 tablespoon vanilla extract
1/2 gallon good-quality vanilla ice cream, softened
Nutmeg

Combine the sugar and water in a stockpot. Cook over medium heat until the sugar is dissolved, stirring constantly. Bring to a boil. Remove the sugar syrup from the heat. Let stand until cool. Combine the bourbon, milk and vanilla in a bowl and mix well. Stir into the syrup. Pour into a sealable freezer bag. Freeze for 8 hours or longer. Place the frozen mixture in a punch bowl and let stand for 1 hour. Add the ice cream and mix with a wooden spoon, breaking up any large pieces. Sprinkle with nutmeg and serve immediately. **Serves 24.**

An East Texas recipe that has become a West Texas holiday tradition.

Almond Lime Punch

1 (6-ounce) package lime gelatin
1 (46-ounce) can pineapple juice
1 (8-ounce) bottle lemon juice
2 1/2 cups sugar
3 cups water
1 ounce almond extract

Dissolve the gelatin in water in a large bowl using the package directions. Add the pineapple juice, lemon juice and sugar and stir until the sugar is dissolved. Add the water and almond extract and stir to mix well. Refrigerate, covered, until chilled. Stir before serving. You may freeze this mixture in a ring mold to make an ice ring. **Serves 25.**

Almond Tea Punch

2 cups sugar
1 quart hot strong tea
2 quarts water
1 tablespoon vanilla extract
1 tablespoon almond extract
1 (6-ounce) can frozen lemonade concentrate
1 (6-ounce) can frozen limeade concentrate
1 (6-ounce) can frozen orange juice concentrate
3 liters ginger ale

Dissolve the sugar in the tea in a pitcher. Add the water, vanilla extract, almond extract, lemonade concentrate, limeade concentrate and orange juice concentrate and mix well. Chill, covered, until serving time. Combine equal portions of the tea mixture and ginger ale in a pitcher and stir to mix. Garnish with citrus slices. You may freeze the tea mixture for future use. **Serves 50.**

Tea bags will stay submerged if you place them in a wire whisk while brewing tea. The whisk can then be used to stir in sugar or any other flavorings added to the tea.

Party Tea

2 quarts water
2 family-size tea bags
1 cup sugar
1 (6-ounce) can frozen lemonade
   concentrate

1 (8-ounce) can pineapple juice
3 or 4 drops of mint extract
Crushed ice

Bring the water to a boil in a saucepan. Add the tea bags and let stand to steep using the package directions. Pour the tea into a 1-gallon pitcher, discarding the tea bags. Add the sugar and stir until dissolved. Prepare the lemonade using the package directions. Add the pineapple juice, lemonade, and mint extract to the tea mixture and stir to mix. Chill, covered, until serving time. Pour over crushed ice in glasses. Garnish each serving with a mint sprig. **Makes 1 gallon.**

Orange Julius

1 (6-ounce) can frozen orange
   juice concentrate
1 cup milk
1 cup water

1/2 cup sugar
1 teaspoon vanilla extract
12 ice cubes

Combine the orange juice concentrate, milk, water, sugar and vanilla in a blender and process for 30 seconds or until blended. Add the ice cubes 1 or 2 at a time, processing constantly. Process until slushy. Pour into glasses and serve. **Serves 4.**

Starters

Appetizers

Tex-Mex on the Plains

Photograph courtesy of Kasey Kearney

A blanket on the ground can be a perfect table setting for a casual summer meal outdoors. Spread talcum powder around the edge of the blanket to keep ants away. Ants will not cross due to the smell and texture of the powder.

Pollo Spiedini

4 boneless skinless chicken breasts
$2/3$ cup bread crumbs
$1/3$ cup grated Parmesan cheese
1 tablespoon chopped fresh Italian parsley
2 teaspoons grated lemon zest
2 garlic cloves, minced
2 tablespoons olive oil
2 tablespoons butter, melted
Juice of 1 lemon

Pound the chicken $1/8$ inch thick between sheets of waxed paper.
Combine the bread crumbs, cheese, parsley, lemon zest and garlic in a
bowl and mix well. Combine the olive oil and butter in a shallow bowl
and mix well.

Dip the chicken into the olive oil mixture, and then coat with the bread
crumb mixture. Roll up the chicken tightly and secure with wooden picks.
Cut into 1-inch pieces and thread onto metal skewers, allowing 4 spirals for
each skewer. Arrange on a foil-lined broiler pan.

Broil 4 inches from the heat source for 4 to 5 minutes per side or until
cooked through. Drizzle with the lemon juice. Remove the skewers from the
chicken before serving. To serve as an entrée, serve with angel hair pasta and
sprinkle with parsley. *Serves 16 as an appetizer or 4 as an entrée.*

Puff Pastry Prosciutto Pinwheels

1 sheet frozen puff pastry, thawed
2 tablespoons honey mustard
4 ounces prosciutto, thinly sliced
1 cup (4 ounces) freshly grated Parmesan cheese
1 egg
2 tablespoons water

Unroll the pastry on a lightly floured work surface, rolling to flatten slightly. Spread the honey mustard over the pastry. Arrange the prosciutto on top of the honey mustard, covering evenly. Sprinkle with the cheese and press into the prosciutto using a rolling pin. Roll as for a jelly roll to enclose half the filling, starting at 1 long end. Repeat the procedure from the remaining long end, brushing with a small amount of water and pressing to seal the rolls together. Cut into 1/2-inch slices and arrange on a lightly greased baking sheet. Chill, covered, for 15 minutes or longer.

Beat the egg and water in a bowl. Brush over the pinwheels. Bake at 400 degrees for 10 minutes or until light golden brown. Serve warm. You may prepare the pinwheels ahead of time and bake just before serving.
Makes 18 to 24 pinwheels.

Oriental Pork Wrappers

12 ounces bulk pork sausage
2 green onions, chopped
1 tablespoon soy sauce
1 tablespoon hoisin sauce
$1/2$ teaspoon minced garlic
24 won ton wrappers

Combine the sausage, green onions, soy sauce, hoisin sauce and garlic in a bowl and mix well. Place a won ton wrapper on a work surface and brush the edges with water. Spoon 1 tablespoon of the sausage mixture onto the center of the wrapper. Bring the edges of the wrapper together over the filling, pressing the seams to seal. Repeat the procedure with the remaining won ton wrappers and filling.

Spray a collapsible steamer with nonstick cooking spray. Arrange a batch of won tons 1 inch apart in the steamer over $1/2$ inch of simmering water. Steam for 8 minutes or until cooked through. Repeat the procedure with the remaining won tons, adding water to the steamer as needed. Serve with soy sauce, hoisin sauce, chili garlic sauce and hot Chinese-style mustard for dipping. **Makes (about) 24 wrappers.**

Lubbock is named after Lieutenant Colonel Thomas S. Lubbock of the Confederate Army.

Crab-Stuffed Mushrooms

12 large mushrooms
Melted butter
Salt and pepper to taste
3 tablespoons minced onion
1 tablespoon olive oil
1 tablespoon unsalted butter
3 tablespoons minced green onions
1 can crab meat, shredded
1/4 cup madeira
3 tablespoons bread crumbs
1/4 cup finely shredded Swiss cheese
1/4 cup grated Parmesan cheese
2 tablespoons minced fresh parsley
1 teaspoon tarragon vinegar
2 to 3 tablespoons heavy cream
Shredded Swiss cheese for sprinkling
Melted butter for drizzling

Remove the stems from the mushrooms and arrange the caps cut side up in a baking dish. Brush with melted butter and sprinkle with salt and pepper. Sauté the onion in the olive oil and 1 tablespoon butter in a skillet until tender; do not brown. Stir in the green onions and crab meat. Remove from the heat. Bring the wine to a boil in a saucepan and boil until almost evaporated. Remove from the heat. Stir in the crab meat mixture, bread crumbs, 1/4 cup Swiss cheese, the Parmesan cheese, parsley and tarragon vinegar. Add just enough cream to moisten and mix well. Fill the mushroom caps with the crab meat mixture. Sprinkle each with a small amount of Swiss cheese and drizzle with melted butter. Bake at 375 degrees for 15 to 20 minutes. Serve immediately. You may substitute chopped mushroom stems for the crab meat. ***Serves 12.***

Bloody Mary Shrimp

1¹/2 pounds boiled peeled shrimp, chopped
2 avocados, coarsely chopped
Juice of 1 lemon
Garlic salt to taste
Chopped green onions to taste
Chopped fresh cilantro to taste
Chopped fresh parsley to taste
1¹/2 tablespoons Worcestershire sauce
2 teaspoons prepared horseradish, or to taste
12 ounces Snap-E-Tom
Salt and pepper to taste

Combine the shrimp and avocado in a bowl. Drizzle with the lemon
juice and sprinkle with garlic salt. Add green onions, cilantro, parsley,
Worcestershire sauce, horseradish and Snap-E-Tom and toss lightly to mix.
Season with salt and pepper. Serve with tortilla chips. You may also serve
as a salad on beds of lettuce. **Serves 12.**

Asparagus Roll-Ups

1 (16-ounce) package thinly sliced ham
8 ounces tub-style whipped cream cheese
1 (12-ounce) jar spicy pickled asparagus spears, drained

Spread 1 ham slice with a small amount of the cream cheese. Place 1 asparagus spear on 1 short side of the ham and roll to enclose, securing with a wooden pick. Repeat with the remaining ham, cream cheese and asparagus. Arrange on a plate and chill, covered, for 1 hour or longer. Cut into bite-size pieces, securing with wooden picks or serve whole. Spicy pickled asparagus spears can be found in the pickle section of the grocery store. *Serves 10 to 12.*

Olive Cheese Balls

1/2 cup (1 stick) margarine, softened
8 ounces sharp Cheddar cheese, finely shredded
1/2 teaspoon Worcestershire sauce
Dash of Tabasco sauce
1 cup plus 2 tablespoons all-purpose flour
60 green olives

Combine the margarine, cheese, Worcestershire sauce and Tabasco sauce in a bowl and mix well. Add the flour and mix well. Shape the dough into 1-inch balls. Poke a hole in each ball and insert an olive into the hole, pressing the dough to enclose. Arrange on a baking sheet. Bake at 350 degrees for 12 to 15 minutes. *Makes 60 appetizers.*

Avocado Cream Potato Skins

6 baking potatoes
6 slices bacon
2 small avocados
1 garlic clove, crushed
2 to 3 teaspoons lemon juice
2 to 3 teaspoons plain yogurt
2 drops of hot red pepper sauce
Salt and pepper to taste
1/4 cup vegetable oil

Prick the potatoes all over with a fork. Bake at 400 degrees for 1 hour.
Remove the potatoes from the oven. Increase the oven temperature to
425 degrees. Cook the bacon in a skillet until crisp; drain. Cut the bacon
into small pieces. Peel the avocados and mash the pulp in a bowl. Stir in
the garlic, lemon juice, yogurt and hot sauce. Season with salt and pepper.
Pour the oil into a roasting pan and place the pan in the oven.

Cut the potatoes lengthwise into halves. Scoop out most of the pulp,
leaving the skins intact and discarding the pulp or reserving for another use.
Sprinkle the potato skins with salt and arrange cut sides down in the hot oil.
Bake for 25 minutes or until golden brown, basting frequently with the oil;
drain. Fill the potato skins with equal portions of the avocado cream.
Arrange the bacon on top. Garnish servings with watercress sprigs. Serve
immediately. ***Serves 4 to 6.***

*Ripe avocados should be
stored at room temperature
and used quickly. Once
peeled, an avocado will
quickly turn black. To avoid
discoloration, add the pit to
the dish until serving time.
Adding lime juice or lemon
juice or placing plastic wrap
directly on the dish will help
retard the discoloration
process. To ripen an avocado
that is too hard or green,
place it in a paper bag with a
banana. The acids in the
banana will help to ripen the
avocado more quickly.*

Pesto, Goat Cheese and Sun-Dried Tomato Torta

1 cup loosely packed fresh basil
1 cup packed spinach, rinsed and stems removed
1 1/2 teaspoons minced garlic
1/4 cup extra-virgin olive oil
1 cup (4 ounces) freshly grated Parmesan cheese
Freshly ground pepper
8 ounces cream cheese, softened
4 ounces goat cheese, softened
1/3 cup drained oil-pack sun-dried tomatoes, minced
1/4 cup finely chopped pine nuts, toasted

Combine the basil, spinach and garlic in a food processor and process until chopped. Add the olive oil gradually, processing constantly. Add the Parmesan cheese and process until blended. Season with pepper. Combine the cream cheese and goat cheese in a bowl and mix until blended and smooth. Line a 3-cup bowl with plastic wrap, leaving a 4-inch overhang.

Shape 1/3 of the cream cheese mixture into a disk and press over the bottom of the prepared bowl. Spread with 1/2 of the basil mixture. Sprinkle with 1/2 of the sun-dried tomatoes and 1/2 of the pine nuts. Repeat the layers of cream cheese mixture, basil mixture, sun-dried tomatoes and pine nuts. Top with the remaining cream cheese mixture, tapping the bowl lightly to allow the ingredients to settle.

Fold the plastic wrap over the top and place in the refrigerator. Let stand for 30 minutes before serving. Invert onto a serving plate, discarding the plastic wrap. Garnish with thinly sliced sun-dried tomatoes. Serve with assorted gourmet crackers. ***Serves 20 to 24.***

Mexican Cheesecake

16 ounces cream cheese, softened
1 egg
1 tablespoon taco seasoning mix
1/2 teaspoon chicken bouillon
   granules
1/4 cup warm water

1 (10-ounce) can chicken, drained
1/2 (4-ounce) can chopped
   green chiles
1 (16-ounce) jar picante sauce
2 cups (8 ounces) shredded
   Cheddar cheese

Combine the cream cheese, egg and taco seasoning mix in a mixing bowl and beat at low speed until mixed. Dissolve the bouillon granules in the water in a bowl. Add to the cream cheese mixture and beat until blended. Mix in the chicken and green chiles. Spoon the cream cheese mixture into a springform pan sprayed with nonstick cooking spray. Bake at 350 degrees for 1 hour or until set. Let stand to cool for 10 to 15 minutes. Remove the side of the pan and place the cheesecake on a serving plate. Pour the picante sauce over the cheesecake and sprinkle with the Cheddar cheese. Serve with tortilla chips. You may serve the cheesecake as an entrée with Spanish rice and tamales. **Serves 36 as an appetizer or 6 as an entrée.**

Triple Cheese Ball

1 jar Roka blue cheese
2 jars Old English cheese
16 ounces cream cheese, softened
1 teaspoon Worcestershire sauce

1 tablespoon dried onion flakes
1/4 cup chopped fresh parsley
1/4 cup chopped nuts

Combine the blue cheese, Old English cheese, cream cheese, Worcestershire sauce and onion flakes in a bowl and mix well. Chill, covered, for 8 to 10 hours. Shape the mixture into a ball. Coat with the parsley and nuts. **Serves 32.**

Feta and Pine Nut Spread

8 ounces tub-style whipped cream cheese
1/2 cup plain nonfat yogurt
3 tablespoons pine nuts, toasted
2 tablespoons chopped fresh basil
1 to 3 garlic cloves, minced
7 ounces feta cheese, crumbled
1/3 cup chopped oil-pack sun-dried tomatoes
Tabasco sauce (optional)

Combine the cream cheese, yogurt, pine nuts, basil and garlic in a food processor and pulse until blended. Add the feta cheese, undrained sun-dried tomatoes and Tabasco sauce and pulse just until chunky. **Serves 20.**

Jalapeño Jelly Cheese Spread

2 cups chopped pecans
2 cups (8 ounces) finely shredded Cheddar cheese
2 bunches green onions including tops, chopped
Mayonnaise
Jalapeño jelly

Combine the pecans, cheese, green onions and enough mayonnaise to moisten in a bowl and mix well. Spoon the pecan mixture into a springform pan sprayed with nonstick cooking spray. Chill, covered, for 8 to 10 hours. Remove the side of the pan and place the cheese spread on a serving plate. Spread with jalapeño jelly. **Serves 32.**

Sensational Shrimp Dip

1 pound shrimp, boiled and peeled
8 ounces cream cheese, chopped
1/2 cup (1 stick) butter, softened
1/2 teaspoon hot red pepper sauce, or to taste
1 tablespoon Worcestershire sauce
1 teaspoon Creole seafood seasoning, or to taste
1 teaspoon lemon juice
1/4 cup finely chopped fresh parsley

Reserve 1/3 of the shrimp. Add 1/2 of the remaining shrimp a few at a time to a food processor, processing constantly. Add 1/3 of the cream cheese and 1/3 of the butter and process until blended. Add the hot sauce, Worcestershire sauce, Creole seasoning and lemon juice and process until puréed. Scrape the bottom and side of the bowl. Add the remaining shrimp, remaining cream cheese and remaining butter 1/2 at a time, processing constantly. Scrape the bottom and side of the bowl. Adjust the seasonings and process for 10 seconds. Spoon into a serving dish and top with the reserved shrimp. Sprinkle with the parsley. Serve with crackers and pita toast. **Serves 20.**

One of the most competitive outdoor sports in West Texas, along with football and golf, is that of outdoor cooking. Although there are two theories as to how to cook on a grill (barbecuing involves a process of slow-cooking and grilling is a method of searing the meat more quickly), both are popular methods for cooking on a warm West Texas evening. The equipment may vary; gas versus charcoal is a common argument. Those who claim to be aficionados of the sport can be very competitive and maintain that practice and patience is the key to success. Although some people in other parts of the country may believe that this is a warm-weather sport, many a chef can be found spending hours outdoors even in the most inclement weather.

Spicy Cold Shrimp Dip

1/2 cup chili sauce
8 ounces cream cheese, softened
1/2 cup mayonnaise-type salad dressing
2 teaspoons prepared horseradish
2 (4-ounce) cans tiny shrimp
1/4 cup chopped onion

Combine the chili sauce and cream cheese in a bowl and mix well. Add the salad dressing, horseradish, shrimp and onion and mix well. Chill, covered, for 1 hour or longer. Serve with chips. **Serves 20.**

Artichoke and Gorgonzola Dip

2 cans artichoke hearts, drained and chopped
2 tablespoons lemon juice
1/4 cup (1/2 stick) butter, melted
1/4 cup Italian-style bread crumbs
8 ounces Gorgonzola cheese, crumbled

Place the artichokes in a 9-inch pie plate and sprinkle with the lemon juice. Drizzle with the butter and sprinkle with the bread crumbs and cheese. Bake at 350 degrees for 20 to 25 minutes or until hot and bubbly. Serve with baguette slices. **Serves 8 to 10.**

Onion Soufflé

4 cups chopped onions
24 ounces cream cheese, softened
2 cups (8 ounces) grated Parmesan cheese
3/4 cup mayonnaise

Combine the onions, cream cheese, Parmesan cheese and mayonnaise in a bowl and mix well. Spoon into a shallow 2-quart baking dish. Bake at 425 degrees for 15 minutes or until golden brown and bubbly. Serve with corn chips. You may use frozen onions in this recipe; thaw on paper towels and press to remove any excess moisture. **Serves 10.**

Blue Cheese and Caramelized Shallot Dip

1 tablespoon vegetable oil
1¼ cups thinly sliced shallots (about 4 ounces)
3/4 cup mayonnaise
3/4 cup sour cream
4 ounces blue cheese, softened
Salt and pepper to taste

Heat the oil in a skillet over medium-high heat. Cook the shallots in the hot oil until dark brown, stirring constantly. Let stand until cool. Combine the mayonnaise, sour cream and blue cheese in a bowl and mix until smooth, pressing with a spatula to remove any lumps. Stir in the shallots, salt and pepper. Chill, covered, for 2 hours or longer to allow the flavors to marry. You may make the dip up to 2 days ahead. **Serves 8.**

The 1015 onion is a sweet, prized onion that is grown in Texas. It was developed by Dr. Leonard Pike of Texas A&M University in the 1980s and was named after the date on which it should be planted, October 15. To remove the smell of onion from your hands, try rubbing them with salt, lemon juice, or the back of a spoon.

Chilled Spinach Dip

2 packages frozen chopped spinach, thawed
2 cups sour cream
2 cups mayonnaise
2 envelopes vegetable soup mix
1/4 cup sliced green onions
1 teaspoon dillweed
1 teaspoon seasoned salt
1/2 teaspoon lemon pepper
3 tablespoons grated Parmesan cheese
2 cups (8 ounces) finely shredded Swiss cheese
2 cans sliced water chestnuts, drained and chopped
1 round loaf sourdough bread

Drain the spinach, squeezing to remove any excess moisture. Combine the sour cream, mayonnaise, soup mix, green onions, dillweed, seasoned salt, lemon pepper, Parmesan cheese and Swiss cheese in a bowl and mix well. Add the spinach and water chestnuts and mix well. Chill, covered, for 24 hours to allow the flavors to marry. Cut a hole in the top of the bread and remove the center of the bread to form a bowl, discarding the removed bread or reserving for another use. Place the bread bowl on a bakng sheet and bake at 150 degrees until toasted. Spoon the dip into the bread bowl. Serve with cocktail bread, crackers or baguette slices. **Serves 24.**

Avocado and Corn Salsa

16 ounces frozen corn kernels, thawed
2 (2-ounce) cans sliced black olives, drained
1 red bell pepper, chopped
1 small onion, chopped
5 garlic cloves, minced
1/3 cup olive oil or vegetable oil
1/4 cup lemon juice
3 tablespoons cider vinegar or white vinegar
1 teaspoon oregano
1/2 teaspoon salt
1/2 teaspoon pepper
4 avocados

Combine the corn, black olives, bell pepper and onion in a bowl and mix well. Combine the garlic, olive oil, lemon juice, vinegar, oregano, salt and pepper in a bowl and mix well. Pour over the corn mixture and toss to coat. Chill, covered, for 8 to 10 hours. Chop the avocados and stir into the salsa just before serving. Serve with tortilla chips. **Serves 50.**

Cranberry Salsa

1 package fresh cranberries
1 bunch green onions, chopped
1 or 2 jalapeño chiles, seeded and minced
1 cup chopped fresh cilantro
3/4 cup sugar
Juice of 1 lime
1 tablespoon olive oil

Process the cranberries in a food processor or blender until ground. Combine the cranberries, green onions, jalapeño chiles and cilantro in a bowl and mix well. Stir in the sugar, lime juice and olive oil. Serve with tortilla chips. **Serves 12.**

To prevent cheese from curdling when heating it for fondues or other sauces, try the following tips:

★ *Use grated or shredded cheese so that it will melt faster, needing less heat.*

★ *Add cornstarch to the cheese before heating it.*

★ *Add lemon juice or wine after the cheese has melted to give some acid to the protein.*

Gazpacho Dip

3 tablespoons olive oil
1 1/2 tablespoons apple
    cider vinegar
3 or 4 avocados, chopped
1 (4-ounce) can chopped
    green chiles

3 or 4 green onions, chopped
1 (4-ounce) can chopped
    black olives
3 or 4 tomatoes, chopped
Garlic salt to taste
Pepper to taste

Combine the olive oil, vinegar, avocados, green chiles, green onions, black olives, tomatoes, garlic salt and pepper in a bowl and mix well. Chill, covered, until serving time. Serve with corn chips. **Serves 16.**

Delicious Dill Dip

1 cup sour cream
1 cup mayonnaise
1 tablespoon Beau Monde seasoning
1 tablespoon dillweed
2 tablespoons finely chopped fresh parsley
2 green onions, minced

Combine the sour cream, mayonnaise, Beau Monde seasoning, dillweed, parsley and green onions in a bowl and mix well. Chill, covered, for 8 to 10 hours to allow the flavors to marry. **Serves 16.**

Creamy Toffee Dip

16 ounces cream cheese, softened
1/3 cup granulated sugar
2/3 cup packed brown sugar
1 teaspoon vanilla extract
1 package toffee bits, or 2 or 3 milk chocolate toffee bars, crushed

Combine the cream cheese, granulated sugar, brown sugar and vanilla in a mixing bowl and beat until blended. Add the toffee bits and mix well. Serve with green apple slices. You may soak the apple slices in pineapple juice to prevent discoloration. **Serves 12.**

Hot Crackers

1 1/2 cups canola oil
1 envelope ranch salad dressing mix
1 tablespoon cayenne pepper
1 (16-ounce) package saltines

Combine the canola oil, salad dressing mix and cayenne pepper in a large container and mix well. Add the crackers and toss to coat; cover. Let stand for 6 hours, occasionally tossing gently. Remove to waxed paper. Let stand until dry. **Serves 30.**

Placing mozzarella cheese in the freezer for about 15 minutes will make it easier to dice.

Seeing Green

Salads

Just for the Ladies

Photograph courtesy of JoDitt Williams

To make sure guests can see each other when seated at a table, scatter a variety of tall, thin items rather than one big centerpiece. For a more formal feel, use candelabra. For a more casual dinner, use a silver tray with a variety of sizes of white candles.

Tequila Bean Salad

SALAD DRESSING

1/4 cup red wine vinegar

2 tablespoons honey

2 tablespoons virgin olive oil

2 ounces tequila

1 (heaping) tablespoon chopped garlic

1/4 cup lime juice

1 tablespoon Worcestershire sauce

Salt and pepper to taste

SALAD

1 cup loosely packed fresh cilantro leaves

1 cup chopped sweet onion

1/2 cup chopped red bell pepper

1 (heaping) tablespoon chopped jalapeño chile

1/3 cup chopped celery

1 (15-ounce) can Great Northern beans, rinsed and drained

1 (15-ounce) can pinto beans, rinsed and drained

1 (15-ounce) can red kidney beans, rinsed and drained

8 tomatoes

FOR THE SALAD DRESSING, combine the vinegar, honey, olive oil, tequila, garlic, lime juice, Worcestershire sauce, salt and pepper in a bowl and mix well.

FOR THE SALAD, combine the cilantro, onion, bell pepper, jalapeño chile, celery, Great Northern beans, pinto beans and kidney beans in a sealable plastic bag. Add the salad dressing. Chill for 1 hour or longer, turning the bag occasionally.

Cut a hole in the top of each tomato and remove the tomato pulp, leaving a shell and reserving the pulp for another use. Spoon equal portions of the salad into each tomato shell. Place each stuffed tomato on an individual salad plate. Garnish with avocado slices, scallions, jalapeño chiles and lime wedges. *Serves 8.*

Cilantro will last longer if you trim the stem ends and wrap it in a damp paper towel. Place it in an unsealed plastic bag and chill.

Mexican Fiesta Salad with Cilantro Salad Dressing

CILANTRO SALAD DRESSING

3 to 5 jalapeño chiles, seeded

1/4 cup white wine vinegar

1 garlic clove

1 teaspoon salt

2/3 cup olive oil

1/2 cup packed fresh cilantro

SALAD

2/3 cup black beans, rinsed and drained

1/2 cup chopped red onion

1 cup corn kernels

1/2 cup chopped green bell pepper

1 1/2 cups seeded chopped tomatoes

2 cups torn lettuce

1 cup (4 ounces) shredded Monterey Jack cheese

1 avocado, cut into 6 slices

4 slices lean bacon, crisp-cooked and crumbled

FOR THE CILANTRO SALAD DRESSING, place the jalapeño chiles, vinegar, garlic and salt in a blender or food processor and process until puréed. Add the olive oil in a fine stream, processing constantly until well mixed. Add the cilantro and process until finely chopped.

FOR THE SALAD, combine the black beans and 2 tablespoons of the Cilantro Salad Dressing in a bowl and mix well. Marinate, covered, for 2 hours or longer. Add the onion and mix well. Combine the corn and bell pepper in a bowl and mix well. Reserve 2 tablespoons of the bean mixture, 1 tablespoon of the tomatoes and 1 tablespoon of the corn mixture. Layer the lettuce, remaining bean mixture, remaining tomatoes, remaining corn mixture and the cheese in a large glass bowl. Arrange the avocado slices on top to resemble the spokes of a wheel. Fill in the spaces between the spokes with the reserved bean mixture, reserved tomatoes, reserved corn mixture and the bacon. Garnish with a cilantro sprig. Serve with the remaining Cilantro Salad Dressing. *Serves 4.*

Broccoli Salad

12 slices bacon
Florets of 2 bunches broccoli, chopped
1 cup chopped celery
$1/2$ cup chopped green onions
1 cup seedless green grapes
1 cup seedless red grapes
$1/2$ cup raisins (optional)
$1/2$ cup blanched slivered almonds
1 cup mayonnaise
1 tablespoon white wine vinegar
$1/4$ cup sugar

Cook the bacon in a skillet over medium-high heat until crisp; drain. Crumble the bacon. Combine the bacon, broccoli, celery, green onions, green grapes, red grapes, raisins and almonds in a bowl and mix well. Whisk the mayonnaise, vinegar and sugar in a bowl. Pour over the salad and toss to coat. Chill, covered, until serving time. *Serves 8.*

Okra Salad

1 large package breaded okra
1 pint cherry tomatoes, cut into halves
1 bunch green onions, chopped
6 slices bacon, crisp-cooked and crumbled
$1/4$ cup vegetable oil
$1/4$ cup sugar
2 tablespoons red wine vinegar or raspberry vinegar

Line a baking sheet with foil and spray the foil with nonstick cooking spray. Place the okra on the prepared baking sheet. Bake at 350 degrees until brown, spraying with nonstick cooking spray every 10 to 15 minutes. Combine the okra, cherry tomatoes, green onions and bacon in a salad bowl and mix gently. Combine the oil, sugar and vinegar in a bowl and mix well. Pour over the okra mixture and toss gently to mix. Serve immediately. *Serves 8 to 10.*

Green and Gold Marinated Salad

3/4 cup vinegar
1/4 cup extra-virgin olive oil
1/4 cup corn oil
1 cup sugar
2 tablespoons water
Salt and pepper to taste
2 cans tiny green peas, drained
2 cans Shoe Peg corn, drained
1 small jar pimento, drained
5 green onions, chopped
6 ribs celery, chopped
1 green bell pepper, chopped

Combine the vinegar, olive oil, corn oil, sugar, water, salt and pepper
in a saucepan. Cook over medium heat until the sugar is dissolved, stirring
frequently. Let stand until cool. Combine the peas, corn, pimento, green
onions, celery and bell pepper in a bowl and mix well. Pour the vinegar
mixture over the vegetable mixture and mix well. Chill, covered, for
12 hours or longer. ***Serves 20.***

July Fourth Potato Salad

3 pounds red potatoes, scrubbed
1 cup Italian salad dressing
4 eggs, hard-cooked
1 cup sliced celery
$1/2$ cup sliced green onions
1 cup mayonnaise
$1/2$ cup sour cream
$1^1/2$ teaspoons horseradish mustard
1 teaspoon garlic salt
1 teaspoon celery seeds

Combine the potatoes and enough water to cover in a saucepan. Cook until tender; drain. Let stand until cool. Slice the potatoes. Combine the potatoes and salad dressing in a bowl and toss to coat. Chill, covered, for 8 to 10 hours. Drain the potatoes. Cut the eggs into halves and separate the egg whites and egg yolks; chop the egg whites. Combine the potatoes, celery, green onions and egg whites in a bowl and mix well. Combine the mayonnaise, sour cream, horseradish mustard, garlic salt and celery seeds in a bowl and mix well. Add to the potato mixture and mix gently. Spoon into a serving dish. Press the egg yolks through a sieve onto the top of the salad. *Serves 8.*

The Spanish explorer Cabeza de Vaca was captured and lived with the Indians off the coast of Texas during the sixteenth century. Pecans used to grow wild along the riverbanks in Texas and Mexico. It is believed that Cabeza de Vaca lived on a diet of mostly pecans during his years in Texas.

Crispy Oriental Salad

1/2 cup (1 stick) butter
2 packages ramen noodles, crushed
1/2 cup sesame seeds
3/4 cup slivered almonds
1 cup sugar
1/2 cup white vinegar
1 cup vegetable oil
1 tablespoon soy sauce
1 large Chinese napa cabbage, chopped
5 green onions with tops, chopped

Melt the butter in a skillet. Reserve the ramen noodle seasoning packet for another use. Add the ramen noodles, sesame seeds and almonds to the skillet and cook until brown, stirring constantly. Combine the sugar, vinegar, oil and soy sauce in a saucepan. Cook until the sugar is dissolved, stirring constantly. Combine the cabbage, green onions and ramen noodle mixture in a bowl and mix well. Stir in the sugar mixture just before serving.
Serves 8.

Stacked Salad

1 head iceberg lettuce, torn
1 cup chopped celery
4 eggs, hard-cooked and sliced
1 (10-ounce) package frozen peas, thawed
1/2 cup chopped green bell pepper
1 small sweet onion, chopped
8 slices bacon, crisp-cooked and crumbled
2 cups mayonnaise
2 tablespoons sugar
1 cup (4 ounces) shredded Cheddar cheese

Layer the lettuce, celery, eggs, peas, bell pepper, onion and bacon in a glass bowl. Combine the mayonnaise and sugar in a bowl and mix well. Spread over the bacon layer. Sprinkle with the cheese. Chill, covered, for 8 to 12 hours. **Serves 8 to 10.**

Butter Lettuce Salad with Avocado, Pine Nuts and Honey Mustard Vinaigrette

HONEY MUSTARD VINAIGRETTE

2 tablespoons white wine vinegar

1 (rounded) tablespoon Dijon mustard

1 tablespoon honey

1 tablespoon olive oil

2 teaspoons crushed garlic

SALAD

1 head butter lettuce, torn

1 green bell pepper, finely chopped

1/2 cup finely chopped red onion

1/4 cup alfalfa sprouts

16 cherry tomatoes, cut into quarters

1/4 cup pine nuts, toasted

1/2 cup (2 ounces) shredded mozzarella cheese

2 tablespoons finely chopped fresh cilantro

1 avocado, chopped

FOR THE HONEY MUSTARD VINAIGRETTE, whisk the vinegar, Dijon mustard, honey, olive oil and garlic in a bowl.

FOR THE SALAD, combine the lettuce, bell pepper, onion, alfalfa sprouts, cherry tomatoes, pine nuts, cheese, cilantro and avocado in a bowl and toss gently to mix. Pour the Honey Mustard Vinaigrette over the salad and toss to coat. Serve immediately. *Serves 4.*

Easter Salad

SALAD DRESSING

1 cup vegetable oil

$^1/3$ cup vinegar

$^3/4$ cup sugar

1 teaspoon salt

1 teaspoon Worcestershire sauce

SALAD

1 head red leaf lettuce, torn

1 head green leaf lettuce, torn

1 pint fresh strawberries, cut into halves

8 ounces seedless green grapes, cut into halves

4 ounces real bacon bits

1 purple onion, chopped

FOR THE SALAD DRESSING, combine the oil, vinegar, sugar, salt and Worcestershire sauce in a bowl and mix well.

FOR THE SALAD, combine the red leaf lettuce, green leaf lettuce, strawberries, grapes, bacon bits and onion in a bowl and mix well. Chill, covered, until serving time. Pour the salad dressing over the salad and toss gently to mix. *Serves 16.*

Autumn Salad with Cinnamon Vinaigrette

Olive oils are graded according to how they are made, based on their color, flavor, aroma, and acidity. They range from olive oil, fino olive oil (fine), virgin olive oil, to extra-virgin olive oil. Extra-virgin olive oil contains only one percent acid and is usually a light golden color. The best olives oils are made from ripe olives that are usually either green or greenish-black.

CINNAMON VINAIGRETTE
1/2 cup raspberry vinegar
1/4 cup sugar
1/2 teaspoon Tabasco sauce
1/2 teaspoon salt
1/4 teaspoon freshly ground pepper
1/2 teaspoon cinnamon
1/2 cup olive oil

SALAD
4 cups torn green leaf lettuce
1 Red Delicious apple, sliced
1/2 cup dried cranberries
1/2 cup sliced honey-roasted almonds

FOR THE CINNAMON VINAIGRETTE, combine the raspberry vinegar, sugar, Tabasco sauce, salt, pepper and cinnamon in a small bowl or jar and mix well. Add the olive oil and whisk until blended.

FOR THE SALAD, combine the lettuce, apple, dried cranberries and almonds in a salad bowl. Drizzle with the desired amount of the Cinnamon Vinaigrette just before serving and toss to coat. Chill any remaining dressing. *Serves 4.*

Cranberry Green Salad

CRANBERRY SALAD DRESSING

1/4 cup frozen cranberry juice concentrate,
   thawed

1/4 cup white wine vinegar

1 1/2 tablespoons Dijon mustard

1/2 tablespoon pepper

1/2 cup vegetable oil

1/4 cup sugar

SALAD

1 1/2 cups dried cranberries

4 cups torn romaine

4 cups torn spinach

1 avocado, chopped

1 small red onion, chopped

1/2 cup sunflower seeds

1/2 cup slivered almonds

FOR THE SALAD DRESSING, combine the cranberry juice concentrate, vinegar, Dijon mustard, pepper, oil and sugar in a jar with a tight-fitting lid and shake until well mixed. Chill until serving time.

FOR THE SALAD, combine the dried cranberries, romaine, spinach, avocado and onion in a salad bowl and toss to mix. Shake the salad dressing. Pour over the salad and toss to coat. Sprinkle with the sunflower seeds and almonds. *Serves 8.*

Mandarin Orange Salad

SALAD DRESSING
1/2 teaspoon salt
Dash of pepper
2 tablespoons sugar
2 tablespoons vinegar
1/4 cup vegetable oil
Dash of hot red pepper sauce
1 tablespoon snipped fresh parsley

SALAD
1/4 cup sliced almonds
1 tablespoon plus 1 teaspoon sugar
1/4 head lettuce, torn
1/4 head romaine, torn
1 cup chopped celery
2 green onions with tops, thinly sliced
1 (11-ounce) can mandarin oranges

FOR THE SALAD DRESSING, combine the salt, pepper, sugar, vinegar, oil, hot sauce and parsley in a jar with a tight-fitting lid and shake to mix. Chill until serving time.

FOR THE SALAD, combine the almonds and sugar in a skillet over low heat. Cook until the sugar is melted and the almonds are coated, stirring constantly. Let stand until cool. Break into small pieces. Combine the lettuce, romaine, celery and green onions in a sealable plastic bag. Chill until serving time.

Add the salad dressing and mandarin oranges to the salad just before serving and shake to coat. Add the almonds and shake to mix. Pour into a salad bowl. You may chill the salad dressing and salad separately for up to 24 hours. ***Serves 4 to 6.***

Chilled Shrimp, Mango and Rice Salad

1/2 cup fat-free mayonnaise
1/2 cup fat-free sour cream
1 teaspoon curry powder
Juice of 1/2 lime
1 1/2 cups chilled cooked rice
1/8 teaspoon cayenne pepper
1/2 cup chopped celery
1 cup sliced water chestnuts, drained

1/2 cup chopped red bell pepper
1/4 cup minced green onions
1 pound cooked peeled shrimp, chilled
2 cups chopped fresh or drained canned mango
Lettuce leaves
1/4 cup sliced almonds, toasted

Combine the mayonnaise, sour cream, curry powder and lime juice in a large bowl and mix well. Add the rice, cayenne pepper, celery, water chestnuts, bell pepper, green onions, shrimp and mango and mix well. Divide among 6 lettuce-lined salad plates and sprinkle with the almonds. **Serves 6.**

Shrimp Louis

1 pound boiled shrimp
3/4 cup (3/4- to 1-inch) celery slices
1/4 cup green salad olives
2 eggs, hard-cooked and grated
3/4 cup chili sauce
1/2 cup mayonnaise-type salad dressing

1 tablespoon chopped onion
1/2 teaspoon sugar or sucralose
1/4 teaspoon Worcestershire sauce
Lemon juice to taste
Salt to taste
Lettuce leaves
Tomato wedges

Cut any large shrimp into halves. Combine the shrimp, celery, olives, eggs, chili sauce, salad dressing, onion, sugar, Worcestershire sauce, lemon juice and salt in a bowl and mix well. Divide among 3 or 4 lettuce-lined salad plates and arrange tomato wedges around the shrimp mixture. You may substitute crab meat for the shrimp. **Serves 3 or 4.**

Chicken Pasta Salad

PARMESAN SALAD DRESSING
1/3 cup grated Parmesan cheese
Garlic paste to taste
Lemon juice
1 envelope zesty Italian salad dressing mix
1/3 cup red wine vinegar
1/4 cup extra-virgin olive oil

SALAD
Zesty Italian salad dressing
1 package boneless skinless chicken breasts
Lemon juice
24 ounces veggie spiral pasta
1 cup chopped carrots
1 cup chopped celery
1 red onion, chopped
1 (2-ounce) can sliced black olives
1 jar pine nuts, toasted
4 ounces feta cheese, crumbled

FOR THE PARMESAN SALAD DRESSING, combine the cheese, garlic paste and enough lemon juice to make of a paste consistency in a bowl and mix well. Combine the cheese mixture, salad dressing mix, vinegar and olive oil in a jar with a tight-fitting lid and shake to mix.

FOR THE SALAD, pour the Italian salad dressing over the chicken in a bowl. Chill, covered, for 8 to 10 hours. Grill or broil the chicken until cooked through, brushing frequently with lemon juice. Chop the chicken. Cook the pasta using the package directions; drain. Combine the chicken, pasta, carrots, celery, onion, black olives, pine nuts and cheese in a bowl and mix well. Add the Parmesan Salad Dressing and toss to coat. Serve immediately. **Serves 8 to 12.**

Rickshaw Salad

SALAD DRESSING

3/4 cup mayonnaise

1/4 cup soy sauce

1 teaspoon hot mustard

1 teaspoon salt

1/2 teaspoon garlic powder

1/4 teaspoon white pepper

SALAD

12 ounces spaghetti

1/2 cup sliced celery

1/2 cup chopped green bell pepper

1/2 cup chopped onion

1/2 cup sliced water chestnuts

4 ounces sliced mushrooms

1 (16-ounce) can bean sprouts, drained

1 cup frozen peas, thawed

FOR THE SALAD DRESSING, combine the mayonnaise, soy sauce, hot mustard, salt, garlic powder and white pepper in a bowl and mix well.

FOR THE SALAD, break the spaghetti into 3-inch pieces. Cook until al dente using the package directions. Sauté the celery, bell pepper, onion, water chestnuts and mushrooms in a skillet until tender. Combine the spaghetti, bean sprouts, peas and celery mixture in a bowl and toss to mix. Add the salad dressing and toss to coat. Chill, covered, for 8 to 10 hours. *Serves 10 to 12.*

Zesty Pasta Salad

1 package multicolor corkscrew pasta
1 can chopped black olives
1 large tomato, chopped
1 package shredded Swiss cheese
1 package sliced honey ham, chopped
1 bottle zesty Italian salad dressing, or to taste

Cook the pasta using the package directions; drain. Combine the pasta, black olives, tomato, cheese, ham and salad dressing in a bowl and mix well. Chill, covered, until serving time. **Serves 10.**

Garden Rice Salad

1 (6-ounce) package long grain and wild rice mix
1/2 cup mayonnaise
1/4 cup plain yogurt
1 cup sliced celery
1 cup chopped tomato
1/2 cup chopped cucumber
2 tablespoons chopped fresh parsley
1/8 teaspoon seasoned salt
1/8 teaspoon pepper
1/4 cup chopped dry roasted peanuts

Cook the rice using the package directions. Let stand until cool. Combine the rice, mayonnaise, yogurt, celery, tomato, cucumber, parsley, seasoned salt and pepper in a bowl and toss lightly to mix. Chill, covered, for 2 to 3 hours. Spoon into a salad bowl. Sprinkle with the peanuts just before serving. **Serves 6 to 8.**

Avocado Ranch Salad Dressing

1 cup mayonnaise
8 ounces guacamole dip
1 cup milk
1 envelope ranch salad dressing mix
1 tablespoon salsa (optional)

Whisk the mayonnaise, guacamole dip, milk, salad dressing mix and salsa in a bowl until well blended. Chill, covered, until serving time. You may serve the salad dressing over a green salad with a Mexican meal. *Makes (about) 3 cups.*

Easy Caesar Salad Dressing

1 small garlic clove
$1/2$ cup mayonnaise
1 tablespoon Worcestershire sauce
3 tablespoons fresh lemon juice
$1/3$ cup olive oil
Salt and pepper to taste

Combine the garlic, mayonnaise, Worcestershire sauce, lemon juice, olive oil, salt and pepper in a blender or food processor and process until smooth. Adjust the seasonings. You may serve the salad dressing over a salad of chopped romaine hearts, croutons and grated Parmesan cheese. Chill any remaining salad dressing. *Makes (about) 1 cup.*

Parmesan Vinaigrette

1/2 cup olive oil
1/4 cup red wine vinegar
1 teaspoon salt
1/2 teaspoon freshly ground pepper
1/4 cup grated Parmesan cheese

Combine the olive oil, vinegar, salt, pepper and cheese in a jar with a tight-fitting lid and shake to mix. You may serve the salad dressing over field greens or any green salad. ***Makes (about) 1 cup.***

Citrus Salad Dressing

1 (6-ounce) can frozen orange juice concentrate, thawed
1 small onion, chopped
1/3 cup red wine vinegar
1 cup packed brown sugar
1 tablespoon grated orange zest
1 teaspoon dry mustard
1 teaspoon salt
1 teaspoon hot red pepper sauce
3 cups olive oil or peanut oil

Combine the orange juice concentrate, onion, vinegar, brown sugar, orange zest, dry mustard, salt, hot sauce and olive oil in a nonaluminum saucepan. Bring to a boil, stirring constantly. Boil for 10 minutes, stirring constantly. Chill, covered, until serving time. You may serve the salad dressing over a salad of spinach and mandarin oranges. ***Makes (about) 5 cups.***

Classic French Dressing

2 teaspoons kosher salt
1 teaspoon freshly cracked
   white pepper
1/2 teaspoon freshly cracked
   black pepper
1/4 teaspoon sugar
1/2 teaspoon dry mustard
1 teaspoon Dijon mustard

1 teaspoon lemon juice
2 teaspoons finely chopped garlic
5 tablespoons tarragon vinegar
2 tablespoons French olive oil
10 tablespoons (about)
   vegetable oil
1 pasteurized egg
1/2 cup light cream

Combine the kosher salt, white pepper, black pepper, sugar, dry mustard, Dijon mustard, lemon juice, garlic, vinegar, olive oil, vegetable oil and egg in a blender. Process for 30 seconds. Add the cream and process just until blended. **Makes (about) 2 cups.**

Cranberry Grape Salad

1 package fresh cranberries
3/4 cup sugar
2 cups seedless red grape halves
1/2 cup broken walnuts or pecans

2 cups miniature marshmallows
1/2 cup heavy whipping cream,
   whipped

Process the cranberries in a food processor or blender until coarsely chopped. Combine the cranberries and sugar in a bowl and mix well. Chill, covered, for 8 to 10 hours. Drain well, pressing lightly to remove any excess liquid. Add the grapes, walnuts and marshmallows and mix well. Fold in the whipped cream just before serving. Serve with poultry or beef. You may use frozen cranberries, add additional grapes and/or omit the walnuts. You may double this recipe. **Serves 6 to 8.**

The Texas High Plains Viticultural area covers 12,000 square miles of the Texas Panhandle and was approved as a grape-growing market in 1993.

Fabulous Fruit Salad

4 cans pineapple tidbits
4 cans mandarin oranges, drained
1 can Bing cherries, drained
2 eggs
2 tablespoons sugar
2 tablespoons lemon juice
1 tablespoon margarine
Dash of salt
1 cup heavy whipping cream
Miniature marshmallows

Drain the pineapple, reserving 2 tablespoons juice. Combine the pineapple, mandarin oranges and Bing cherries in a bowl and mix well. Combine the eggs, sugar, lemon juice, reserved pineapple juice, margarine and salt in a saucepan. Bring to a boil over low heat, stirring constantly. Remove from the heat. Let stand until completely cool. Beat the whipping cream in a bowl until stiff peaks form. Fold into the egg mixture. Pour over the pineapple mixture and mix gently. Fold in the marshmallows. Chill, covered, until serving time. **Serves 40.**

Blueberry Holiday Salad

2 (3-ounce) packages black cherry gelatin or
   blackberry gelatin
2 cups boiling water
1 (15-ounce) can blueberries
1 (8-ounce) can crushed pineapple
$1/2$ cup sugar
1 cup sour cream
8 ounces cream cheese, softened
$1/2$ teaspoon vanilla extract
$1/2$ cup chopped pecans

Dissolve the gelatin in the boiling water in a bowl. Drain the blueberries and pineapple, reserving the juice in a 1-cup measure. Add enough water to the reserved juice to measure 1 cup. Add to the gelatin and mix well. Stir in the blueberries and pineapple. Pour into a 2-quart rectangular dish. Chill, covered, until set. Combine the sugar, sour cream, cream cheese and vanilla in a bowl and mix well. Spread over the gelatin mixture. Sprinkle with the pecans. *Serves 8.*

Cranberry and Pineapple Congealed Salad

1 (12-ounce) package fresh cranberries
1/2 cup sugar
3 (3-ounce) packages raspberry or mixed berry gelatin
2 cups boiling water
2 cups cranberry juice
1 (8-ounce) can crushed pineapple
1 cup chopped celery
2/3 cup chopped pecans, toasted

Process the cranberries in a food processor or blender until chopped. Combine the cranberries and sugar in a bowl and mix well. Dissolve the gelatin in the boiling water in a bowl. Stir in the cranberry juice. Chill, covered, for 30 minutes. Add the cranberry mixture, pineapple, celery and pecans and mix well. Pour into a greased bundt pan. Chill, covered, for 8 hours. Invert onto a serving plate. **Serves 10 to 12.**

Lemon Raspberry Layered Salad

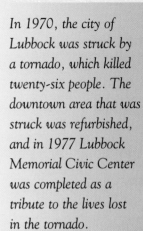

1 (15-ounce) can crushed pineapple
1 (3-ounce) package lemon gelatin
1¹/2 cups miniature marshmallows
8 ounces cream cheese, softened
1 cup heavy whipping cream
2 tablespoons sugar
1/4 teaspoon vanilla extract
2 (3-ounce) packages raspberry gelatin
2 cups boiling water
16 ounces frozen raspberries

Drain the pineapple, reserving the juice in a 1-cup measure. Add enough water to the reserved juice to measure 1 cup. Bring to a boil in a saucepan. Add the lemon gelatin and stir until dissolved. Combine the marshmallows and cream cheese in a large bowl. Add the hot lemon gelatin mixture and stir until the cream cheese is melted and the mixture is smooth. Beat the whipping cream in a bowl until stiff peaks form. Beat in the sugar and vanilla. Add to the marshmallow mixture and stir to mix well. Fold in the pineapple. Pour into a 9×13-inch serving dish. Chill, covered, until set. Dissolve the raspberry gelatin in the boiling water in a bowl. Let stand until cool. Stir in the undrained raspberries. Spoon over the congealed layer. Chill, covered, until set. **Serves 12 to 14.**

In 1970, the city of Lubbock was struck by a tornado, which killed twenty-six people. The downtown area that was struck was refurbished, and in 1977 Lubbock Memorial Civic Center was completed as a tribute to the lives lost in the tornado.

Terrific Tureens

Soups

An Evening to Remember

Photograph courtesy of Ann McDonald

Soups or dips can be served in bowls made from bread. Hollow out the insides of round loaves of bread and fill with soup. Your guests can dip the bread pieces into the soup and then eat the bowl when the soup is gone.

Texas Posole

2 pounds ground beef
1 onion, chopped
1 small can chopped green chiles
1 envelope taco seasoning mix
1 envelope ranch salad
    dressing mix
Salt and pepper to taste
Sugar to taste

3 cans stewed tomatoes
1 can hominy, drained
1 can kidney beans
1 can pinto beans
Shredded cheese
Chopped avocado
Lime slices

Posole is an ancient dish from Jalisco, Mexico, and is served at Christmas and on certain feast days. It is a simple and tasty dish that fills the kitchen with the savory aroma of the Southwest.

Brown the ground beef with the onion in a saucepan, stirring until crumbly; drain. Add the green chiles, taco seasoning mix, salad dressing mix, salt, pepper, sugar, tomatoes, hominy, undrained kidney beans and undrained pinto beans and mix well. Cook over low heat for 30 minutes. Ladle into soup bowls. Top with cheese, chopped avocado and lime slices. ***Serves 8 to 10.***

Posole Rojo

3 tablespoons olive oil
1 large onion, chopped
2 carrots, sliced
3 ribs celery, chopped
3 pounds bone-in country-style
    pork ribs

2 large cans hominy
1 tablespoon ground cumin
3 tablespoons chili powder
1 teaspoon salt
1 teaspoon pepper

Heat the olive oil in a stockpot. Sauté the onion, carrots and celery in the hot oil until the onion is translucent. Add the ribs and enough water to cover. Cook, covered, over medium heat for 1 hour to make a stock. Strain the stock into a saucepan, reserving the ribs. Let the ribs stand until cool. Remove and discard the bones from the ribs and chop the pork into bite-size pieces. Chill the stock, covered, until the fat rises to the top. Skim and discard the fat. Bring the stock to a boil. Add the chopped pork, hominy, cumin, chili powder, salt and pepper and mix well. Simmer for 1 hour, stirring occasionally. Ladle into soup bowls. ***Serves 8.***

Green Chile Stew

1¹/₂ pounds (1-inch) pork cubes
3 Yukon gold potatoes
1 yellow onion
1 (12-ounce) can beef broth
¹/₈ teaspoon garlic powder
¹/₄ teaspoon salt
¹/₄ teaspoon pepper

1 (12-ounce) can whole tomatoes
8 ounces roasted and peeled fresh
    green chiles, chopped
Shredded Cheddar cheese
    (optional)
8 flour tortillas, warmed (optional)

Cook the pork in a skillet just until brown, stirring frequently. Cut the potatoes and onion into bite-size pieces. Combine the pork, potatoes and onion in a slow cooker and mix well. Add the beef broth, garlic powder, salt and pepper. Chop the tomatoes, reserving the juice. Add the tomatoes, reserved juice and green chiles to the pork mixture and mix well. Add enough water to fill the slow cooker. Cook on High for 1 to 1¹/₂ hours; stir. Cook for 3 to 3¹/₂ hours longer. Adjust the seasonings. Ladle into soup bowls. Sprinkle each serving with Cheddar cheese and top each with a warm tortilla. **Serves 8.**

Tamale Soup

¹/₂ cup finely chopped onion
1 teaspoon minced garlic
2 cans chicken broth
12 tamales
1 large can mild red
    enchilada sauce

1 teaspoon chili powder
¹/₂ teaspoon ground cumin, or
    to taste
1 small package Velveeta cheese,
    cubed
Shredded cheese

Combine the onion, garlic and 1 can of the chicken broth in a stockpot. Cook until heated through, stirring occasionally. Add the tamales. Cook just until the tamales begin to crumble. Stir in 1 broth can water. Bring to a simmer. Mash the tamales with a potato masher. Add the remaining 1 can chicken broth, the enchilada sauce and 1 enchilada sauce can water and mix well. Add the chili powder and cumin. Cook until heated through, stirring frequently; do not boil. Add the cheese and cook until melted, stirring constantly; do not burn. Cook for 30 minutes, stirring occasionally and adding additional water if needed. Ladle into soup bowls. Sprinkle with shredded cheese. Serve with tortilla chips. **Serves 10.**

Santa Fe Corn Soup

3¹/2 cups frozen corn kernels

1 cup chicken broth

¹/4 cup (¹/2 stick) butter or
    margarine

2 cups milk, or 1 cup evaporated
    milk plus 1 cup water

1 garlic clove, minced

1 teaspoon oregano

Salt and pepper to taste

3 tablespoons canned green chiles,
    rinsed, drained and chopped

1 cup chopped cooked chicken

1 cup (4 ounces) shredded
    Monterey Jack cheese

¹/4 teaspoon baking soda

1 cup chopped tomatoes

Combine the corn and chicken broth in a blender or food processor and process until puréed. Combine the corn mixture and butter in a 3-quart saucepan. Bring to a simmer, stirring constantly. Simmer for 5 minutes, stirring constantly. Add the milk, garlic, oregano, salt and pepper and mix well. Bring to a boil. Reduce the heat. Add the green chiles and chicken. Simmer for 5 minutes, stirring frequently. Remove from the heat. Add the cheese and baking soda and cook until the cheese is melted, stirring constantly. Ladle into soup bowls. Top with equal portions of the tomatoes. Garnish each serving with a fried tortilla triangle and a sprig of fresh oregano. ***Serves 6.***

Chicken Enchilada Soup

2 tablespoons margarine

1 small onion, chopped

1 teaspoon paprika

1 teaspoon chili powder

¹/4 teaspoon salt

¹/2 teaspoon ground cumin

1 garlic clove, minced

¹/2 cup all-purpose flour

2 cups sour cream

2 quarts water

1 bunch green onions, chopped

2 tablespoons chicken
    bouillon granules

2 cups (8 ounces) shredded
    Cheddar cheese

1 (4-ounce) can chopped
    green chiles

3 cups chopped cooked chicken

Melt the margarine in a stockpot. Sauté the onion in the margarine until translucent. Add the paprika, chili powder, salt, cumin, garlic and flour and mix well. Add the sour cream and water gradually, stirring constantly. Stir in the green onions, bouillon, cheese, green chiles and chicken. Simmer for 30 minutes, stirring occasionally. Serve immediately or chill, covered, until serving time and reheat. ***Serves 10.***

Chicken Tortilla Soup

2 tablespoons unsalted butter
1 cup fresh corn kernels
4 garlic cloves, minced
1 cup chopped onion
1 cup chopped celery
1/2 cup chopped carrots
2 large Anaheim chiles, seeded and chopped
1 tablespoon ground cumin
1 teaspoon chili powder
1 1/2 teaspoons oregano
1 1/2 cups diced tomatoes
1 quart chicken broth
1 bunch cilantro, chopped
2 cups shredded rotisserie chicken
1 1/2 tablespoons kosher salt
1 1/2 teaspoons freshly ground pepper
2 cups broken tortilla chips
1 avocado, chopped
1 cup (4 ounces) shredded Monterey Jack cheese

The difference in salts is not in their chemical makeup, but rather in their texture. Table salt will have the finest granules, making it easier to use for baking. Sea salt and kosher salt have larger, uneven grains, and many cooks prefer a larger grain for flavoring meats and other dishes. Table salt is made from underground salt deposits, but sea salt is made from evaporated seawater. Kosher salt can be derived from either seawater or underground sources. Its name comes from the way it is processed. Because it contains no preservatives, it is sometimes used in preserving foods.

Melt the butter in a saucepan over medium heat. Cook the corn, garlic, onion, celery, carrots and chiles in the butter for 3 minutes, stirring occasionally. Add the cumin, chili powder and oregano. Cook for 3 minutes, stirring constantly. Add the tomatoes, chicken broth, cilantro and chicken. Bring to a boil. Reduce the heat and simmer for 10 minutes. Season with the kosher salt and pepper. Divide the tortilla chips among 10 soup bowls. Ladle the soup into the bowls. Sprinkle with equal portions of the avocado and cheese. **Serves 10.**

Creamy Chicken and Potato Soup

¹/4 cup vegetable oil
4 cups chopped potatoes
1 onion, chopped
1¹/2 to 2 cups chopped or
   shredded cooked chicken
   (preferably white meat)

1 cup chicken broth
2 teaspoons parsley flakes
2 teaspoons salt
Dash of pepper
1 (12-ounce) can evaporated milk

Heat the oil in a saucepan. Add the potatoes and onion and toss to coat. Add the chicken, chicken broth, parsley, salt and pepper. Bring to a boil, stirring occasionally. Reduce the heat. Simmer, covered, until the potatoes are tender, about 30 minutes. Stir in the evaporated milk and cook until heated through. Ladle into soup bowls. ***Serves 6.***

Corn and Crab Bisque

4 cups milk
4 cups heavy cream
1 cup chicken broth
¹/4 cup (¹/2 stick) butter
¹/4 cup all-purpose flour
24 ounces canned corn

1 pound crab meat, flaked
2 cups chopped green onions
Salt and pepper to taste
1 tablespoon chopped
   fresh parsley

Bring the milk, cream and chicken broth to a boil in a saucepan. Reduce the heat and simmer for 10 to 12 minutes. Combine the butter and flour in a saucepan. Cook until brown, stirring constantly. Add to the milk mixture and mix well. Stir in the undrained corn and crab meat. Simmer for 5 minutes, stirring frequently. Add 1 cup of the green onions and mix well. Season with salt and pepper. Ladle into soup bowls. Sprinkle with equal portions of the parsley and the remaining 1 cup green onions. ***Serves 6 to 8.***

Lobster Bisque

1 cup chopped onion
$^1/_2$ cup (1 stick) butter or margarine
$^1/_4$ cup all-purpose flour
6 cups chicken broth
1 cup cracker crumbs
4 to 6 cups fresh or frozen lobster tails
2 teaspoons curry powder
2 cups cream
Pepper to taste
1 can condensed tomato soup

Sauté the onion in the butter in a saucepan for 10 minutes. Remove from the heat. Stir in the flour. Add 3 cups of the chicken broth gradually, stirring constantly. Add the cracker crumbs and mix well. Process in batches in a blender or food processor until blended and smooth. Return to the saucepan. Add the remaining 3 cups chicken broth. Bring to a boil. Reduce the heat. Remove the meat from the lobster tails. Add the lobster meat to the soup and cook for 5 minutes. Stir in the curry powder, cream and pepper and cook just until heated through. Stir in the tomato soup and cook just until heated through. Ladle into soup bowls. **Serves 8 to 10.**

Asparagus Bisque

4^1/$_2$ cups water
2 large leeks including pale green tops,
    cut into halves and thinly sliced
1 teaspoon curry powder
2^1/$_2$ pounds asparagus, trimmed and
    cut into 1-inch pieces
1 cup crème fraîche or sour cream
^{1}/$_4$ cup chopped fresh dillweed
1 teaspoon curry powder
^{3}/$_4$ teaspoon salt, or to taste
^{1}/$_2$ teaspoon pepper, or to taste
2 tablespoons chopped fresh dillweed

Bring the water, leeks and 1 teaspoon curry powder to a boil in a saucepan
over medium heat. Boil for 5 minutes. Add the asparagus. Reduce the heat
to medium. Simmer, covered, for 15 minutes or until the asparagus is tender.
Let stand for 15 to 20 minutes to cool. Add the crème fraîche, ^{1}/$_4$ cup
dillweed and 1 teaspoon curry powder. Process in batches in a blender until
puréed. Season with the salt and pepper. Chill, covered, for 4 to 10 hours.
Ladle into soup bowls and sprinkle with equal portions of the 2 tablespoons
dillweed. ***Serves 6.***

Texas farmers grow over one hundred varieties of chiles, from mild to blistering.

Jalapeño Bisque

1/4 cup (1/2 stick) unsalted butter
6 jalapeño chiles, seeded, deveined and minced
1 small red onion, minced
3 garlic cloves, minced
1 avocado, chopped
2 cups chopped tomatoes

8 cups heavy cream or half-and-half
Kosher salt to taste
Freshly ground pepper to taste
Leaves of 1 bunch cilantro, chopped

Melt the butter in a heavy saucepan over medium heat. Sauté the jalapeño chiles, onion and garlic in the hot butter until tender. Remove from the heat. Stir in the avocado, tomatoes and cream. Reduce the heat to low and return the saucepan to the heat. Bring to a simmer, stirring constantly. Cook for 30 minutes or until reduced by 1/3, stirring occasionally; do not burn. Season with kosher salt and pepper. Reserve a small amount of the cilantro. Stir the remaining cilantro into the soup just before serving. Ladle into soup bowls and sprinkle with the reserved cilantro. **Serves 6.**

Butternut Squash Bisque

2 tablespoons butter or margarine
2 small onions, minced
3 cups peeled seeded chopped butternut squash
1 1/4 quarts chicken broth

1 1/2 cups chopped potatoes
1 teaspoon paprika
1/2 cup heavy cream
Salt and freshly ground pepper to taste

Melt the butter in a saucepan. Cook the onions in the hot butter for 5 minutes or until tender. Add the squash, chicken broth, potatoes and paprika and mix well. Bring to a boil. Reduce the heat to low. Simmer, covered, for 35 minutes or until the squash is tender. Process in batches in a food processor or blender until smooth. Return the soup to the saucepan. Stir in the cream. Season with salt and pepper. Cook over low heat until heated through. Ladle into soup bowls. Garnish with snipped fresh chives and whole chives. **Serves 8 to 10.**

Roasted Garlic Soup

4 garlic bulbs
$^1/4$ cup olive oil
$^1/4$ cup dried onion flakes
$^2/3$ cup water
$^1/2$ cup (1 stick) butter
$^1/2$ cup all-purpose flour
3 (14-ounce) cans chicken broth, heated
$^1/3$ cup dry sherry
2 cups heavy cream
Lemon juice to taste
Salt to taste
White pepper to taste
2 tablespoons chopped fresh chives

Cut $^1/4$ inch off the top of the garlic bulbs. Arrange cut sides up in a shallow baking dish. Drizzle with the olive oil and cover loosely with foil. Bake at 350 degrees for 1 hour and 15 minutes or until golden brown. Let stand until slightly cool. Press the cloves onto a cutting board. Chop the garlic. Soak the onion flakes in $^2/3$ cup water; drain. Melt the butter in a heavy saucepan over medium heat. Sauté the garlic and onion flakes in the hot butter for 8 minutes. Reduce the heat to low. Add the flour and cook for 10 minutes, stirring occasionally. Stir in the chicken broth and sherry. Simmer for 20 minutes, stirring occasionally. Let stand until slightly cool. Process in batches in a blender or food processor until puréed. You may chill the mixture, covered, until ready to proceed. Pour the mixture into a saucepan. Add the cream and simmer for 10 minutes or until thickened. Stir in lemon juice, salt and white pepper. Ladle into soup bowls and sprinkle with the chives. **Serves 4.**

Chilled Green Chile Soup

1 1/2 cups chicken broth
1/4 cup minced onion
3 ounces cream cheese, softened
1 cup sour cream
2 (4-ounce) cans chopped green chiles
1/4 teaspoon ground cumin
1 teaspoon minced garlic
1 cup heavy cream
1/2 teaspoon salt

Bring the chicken broth and onion to a boil in a saucepan. Reduce the heat and simmer for 5 minutes. Let stand until cool. Combine the cream cheese and sour cream in a bowl and mix well. Add the green chiles, cumin and garlic and mix well. Stir in the chicken broth mixture, cream and salt. Process in batches in a blender until smooth. Chill, covered, until serving time or for up to 1 week. **Serves 4.**

French Onion Soup

3 tablespoons extra-virgin olive oil
4 onions, thinly sliced
1/4 tablespoon freshly ground pepper
2 garlic cloves, chopped
1/2 teaspoon thyme
6 cups beef broth
4 slices French bread, toasted
3/4 cup (3 ounces) shredded Gruyère cheese

Heat the olive oil in a heavy saucepan over low heat. Cook the onions and pepper in the hot oil for 30 minutes or until golden brown, stirring occasionally. Add the garlic and thyme and mix well. Cook for 2 minutes, stirring occasionally. Add the beef broth. Bring to a boil. Reduce the heat and simmer, covered, for 30 minutes. Ladle into 4 ovenproof soup bowls. Place a bread slice on top of each serving and sprinkle with equal portions of the cheese. Broil until the cheese is melted and the top is brown. **Serves 4.**

Potato Soup

24 ounces frozen cubed hash
    brown potatoes
3 cups water
1 onion, chopped
1 (10-ounce) can condensed
    cream of celery soup
1 cup milk
1 cup half-and-half

1 tablespoon margarine
1 teaspoon salt
1 teaspoon pepper
3 garlic cloves, minced (optional)
Bacon bits
Shredded cheese
Green onion tops

Bring the potatoes, water and onion to a simmer in a stockpot. Simmer for 7 to 10 minutes or until heated through. Add the cream of celery soup, milk, half-and-half, margarine, salt, pepper and garlic and mix well. Cook for 8 to 10 minutes, stirring occasionally. Ladle into soup bowls. Top each serving with bacon bits, cheese and green onion tops. ***Serves 8 to 10.***

Garden Gazpacho

1/2 teaspoon basil
1/2 teaspoon oregano
1/4 teaspoon thyme
1 (28-ounce) can diced tomatoes
1 large cucumber, or 2 medium
    cucumbers, seeded and chopped
2 large avocados, chopped
2 garlic cloves, crushed
1 onion, finely chopped

1/4 cup good-quality olive oil
2 tablespoons red wine vinegar
1/4 cup fresh lime juice, or
    2 tablespoons fresh lemon juice
Salt and pepper to taste
1 (46-ounce) can tomato juice
Croutons (optional)
Chopped fresh parsley

Rub the basil, oregano and thyme between fingers to crush. Combine the tomatoes, cucumber, avocados, garlic, onion, olive oil, vinegar, lime juice, salt, pepper, basil, oregano, thyme and tomato juice in a jar with a tight-fitting lid and mix well. Chill, covered, for 5 to 6 hours or until well chilled. Ladle into soup bowls. Top with croutons and parsley. ***Serves 8 to 10.***

Tomato Basil Soup

6 tablespoons unsalted butter
1 tablespoon finely chopped onion, or
    1 tablespoon onion powder
1 (28-ounce) can tomato purée
2 cups chicken broth
2 cups milk
1 small bunch basil
1 cup sour cream
1 cup (4 ounces) freshly grated Parmesan cheese

Melt the butter in a large saucepan or Dutch oven. Sauté the onion in the hot butter for 2 to 3 minutes or until tender. Add the tomato purée, chicken broth, milk and basil and mix well. Simmer for 30 minutes, stirring occasionally.

Combine 1 cup of the soup and the sour cream in a blender or food processor and process until smooth. Whisk the sour cream mixture into the remaining soup and cook just until heated through; do not boil. Stir in the cheese just before serving. ***Serves 6.***

Vegetable Cheese Soup

1/2 cup grated carrots
1/2 cup finely chopped celery
1 cup finely chopped scallions
1 cup finely chopped broccoli
6 cups chicken broth
1/2 cup (1 stick) margarine
1 onion, chopped
1 cup all-purpose flour
4 cups milk
1 (15-ounce) jar Cheez Whiz
1 teaspoon prepared mustard
Salt and pepper to taste

Bring the carrots, celery, scallions, broccoli and chicken broth to a boil in a stockpot. Boil for 5 minutes. Let stand until slightly cool. Melt the margarine in a saucepan. Sauté the onion in the hot margarine until tender. Add the flour and stir until a paste forms. Add the milk to the carrot mixture and mix well. Add the flour mixture gradually, whisking constantly. Bring to a boil. Reduce the heat. Add the Cheez Whiz, prepared mustard, salt and pepper and cook until heated through. Ladle into soup bowls. This soup freezes well. **Serves 12 to 15.**

The Main Event

Entrées and Main Dishes

Home for the Holidays: A Grand Buffet

Photograph courtesy of JoDitt Williams

Red glass bowls and platters are great for all your red summer and winter holidays, including Christmas, Valentine's Day, July Fourth, and Memorial Day. Just change the accent color to match each holiday.

Best Oven Brisket

1 (4- to 5-pound) beef brisket
1 can beef consommé
1 (5-ounce) bottle light soy sauce
1 tablespoon liquid smoke
1/4 cup lemon juice
2 tablespoons minced garlic

Place the brisket in a nonreactive baking dish. Combine the beef consommé, soy sauce, liquid smoke, lemon juice and garlic in a bowl and mix well. Pour over the brisket. Chill, covered, for 8 to 10 hours. Bake, covered, at 300 degrees for 1 hour per pound, turning and basting frequently with the marinade. Uncover and increase the oven temperature to 325 degrees for the last 30 minutes of the baking time. You may instead bake the brisket all day at 275 degrees. **Serves 10 to 12.**

Beef Teriyaki with Broccoli

1 cup beef broth
1/3 cup teriyaki sauce
1 tablespoon cornstarch
1/4 teaspoon red pepper flakes
1 garlic clove, crushed
1 tablespoon vegetable oil
1 pound filets mignons, cut into strips
3 cups broccoli florets
1 cup red bell pepper strips
Hot cooked rice or Chinese noodles

Combine the beef broth, teriyaki sauce, cornstarch, red pepper flakes and garlic in a bowl and mix well. Heat the oil in a nonstick skillet or wok over medium-high heat. Stir-fry the beef in the hot oil for 3 minutes. Add the broccoli and bell pepper and stir-fry for 3 minutes. Add the broth mixture. Cook for 3 minutes or until thickened. Serve over rice. You may add water chestnuts or mandarin oranges to the stir-fry. **Serves 4.**

For success in marinating:

★ *Always marinate beef in the refrigerator and not at room temperature.*

★ *Tender cuts of beef need only be marinated for fifteen minutes to two hours for flavor.*

★ *Less tender cuts should be marinated for at least six hours in a mixture containing a food acid or enzyme.*

★ *Marinating longer than twenty-four hours may cause meat to become soft or mushy.*

★ *Never save or reuse marinade. If it is to be used later for basting or as a sauce, reserve a portion before adding to the meat.*

★ *Marinate in a plastic bag or glass container that will not react to the marinade.*

—Texas Beef Council

Carne Guisada (Stewed Meat)

2 pounds sirloin steak
2 tablespoons canola oil
1/2 onion, chopped
2 garlic cloves, minced
1 green bell pepper, chopped
1 jalapeño chile, minced
3 tomatoes, chopped

1 can tomato sauce
1 teaspoon salt
1/2 teaspoon black pepper
2 teaspoons ground cumin
1/4 teaspoon chili powder
1/4 teaspoon cayenne pepper
1 cup (about) water or beef stock

Cut the steak into 1-inch pieces. Heat the canola oil in a skillet over medium heat. Brown the steak in the hot oil, stirring occasionally. Stir in the onion, garlic, bell pepper and jalapeño chile. Cook for 15 to 20 minutes or until brown, stirring frequently. Add the tomatoes, tomato sauce, salt, black pepper, cumin, chili powder and cayenne pepper and mix well. Stir in enough of the water to make of the desired consistency. Simmer for 20 to 30 minutes, stirring occasionally. Serve with flour tortillas. You may substitute 1 large can tomatoes, undrained, for the tomatoes and tomato sauce. **Serves 4.**

Beef Ragout

1 (3¹/2-pound) round steak
   (about 1¹/2 inches thick)
1/2 cup all-purpose flour
1¹/2 tablespoons salt
1¹/2 teaspoons pepper
1/4 cup vegetable oil
2 cups sliced onions

2 cans condensed tomato soup
1 tomato soup can water
8 new potatoes, scrubbed, or
   3 potatoes, chopped
6 carrots, cut into quarters
2 packages frozen green peas

Cut the steak into serving pieces. Combine the flour, salt and pepper and mix well. Pound the flour mixture into the steak. Heat the oil in a skillet. Brown the steak in the hot oil, stirring frequently. Add the onions and cook until light brown, stirring frequently. Add the soup and water and mix well. Simmer, covered, for 2 hours. Add the potatoes and carrots and mix well. Simmer, covered, until the steak and vegetables are tender. Stir in the green peas and cook until heated through. Serve with a green salad and French bread. **Serves 8 to 10.**

Schweitzer Chili

12 ounces chorizo

2 tablespoons olive oil

2 pounds sirloin steak, cut into 1-inch pieces

8 ounces ground beef

1 large yellow onion, coarsely chopped

2 jalapeño chiles

1/4 cup chili powder

1 tablespoon garlic salt

2 teaspoons ground cumin

1 teaspoon basil

2 (14-ounce) cans beef broth

2 (14-ounce) cans diced tomatoes

1 cup chopped fresh cilantro

1 cinnamon stick

3 bay leaves

1 tablespoon yellow cornmeal

Salt and pepper to taste

Shredded Cheddar cheese

Sour cream

In Sandpoint, Idaho, in the late nineteenth century, it is believed that there lived a Mr. Schweitzer in a primitive cabin at the base of Schweitzer Mountain Resort. He was of Swiss origin and was considered to be somewhat eccentric. After he displayed some bizarre behavior, they found a grisly discovery inside his cabin. He had accumulated the hides of several missing pets in the area. After that, he was taken to an insane asylum and was never seen around Sandpoint again.

Remove the casings from the sausage and cut the sausage into 1/2-inch pieces. Heat the olive oil in a heavy stockpot over medium heat. Brown the steak in batches in the hot oil, stirring frequently. Remove to a bowl using a slotted spoon. Brown the ground beef and sausage with the onion in the drippings, stirring until crumbly; drain. Return the steak to the stockpot and mix well. Cut 3 lengthwise slits in each jalapeño chile. Add the jalapeño chiles, chili powder, garlic salt, cumin, basil, beef broth, tomatoes, cilantro, cinnamon stick, bay leaves, cornmeal, salt and pepper to the steak mixture and mix well. Bring to a boil. Reduce the heat and simmer for 2 hours, stirring occasionally. Remove and discard the cinnamon stick, bay leaves and jalapeño chiles. Ladle the soup into soup bowls. Sprinkle with cheese and top with sour cream. **Serves 8.**

Beef Viennese

2 pounds ground round
1/4 cup milk
1/4 cup bread crumbs
1 egg
1/2 teaspoon salt
1/2 teaspoon pepper
1/4 cup (1/2 stick) butter
2 cups sliced onions
2 tablespoons all-purpose flour
3 tablespoons tomato paste
2 cups boiling water
2 beef bouillon cubes
Garlic powder to taste
1 cup sour cream
8 ounces egg noodles
1/4 cup (1/2 stick) butter
Poppy seeds to taste

Braising is a cooking method that helps tenderize less tender cuts of meat, such as brisket. It usually involves browning the meat, then deglazing, and finally simmering the meat for a period of time.

Combine the ground beef, milk, bread crumbs, egg, salt and pepper in a bowl and mix well. Shape into 2-inch patties. Melt 1/4 cup butter in a skillet over medium-high heat. Sauté the onions in the hot butter until tender. Remove to a plate using a slotted spoon. Brown the ground beef patties on both sides in the pan drippings. Remove to a plate using a slotted spoon. Add the flour to the pan drippings and mix well. Stir in the tomato paste. Add the water and bouillon cubes and cook until the bouillon cubes are dissolved, stirring constantly. Reduce the heat. Add the sautéed onions, ground beef patties and garlic powder. Simmer for 40 minutes or until the ground beef patties are cooked through, stirring occasionally. Stir in the sour cream just before serving. Cook the noodles using the package directions; drain. Add 1/4 cup butter and poppy seeds to the hot noodles and toss to coat. Serve the beef mixture over the noodles on a platter. ***Serves 8.***

Marvelous Meat Loaf

2 pounds ground beef
1 teaspoon salt
1/2 teaspoon pepper
2 eggs, lightly beaten
1/4 cup chopped onion

1 tablespoon prepared mustard
1/4 cup packed brown sugar
1 small can tomato sauce
12 crackers, crushed

Combine the ground beef, salt and pepper in a bowl and mix well. Add the eggs, onion, mustard, brown sugar and tomato sauce and mix well. Add the crackers and mix well. Shape into a loaf and place in a 9×9-inch baking dish. Bake at 350 degrees for 45 to 60 minutes or until cooked through. You may sprinkle shredded cheese on top or spread with additional tomato sauce 10 minutes before the end of the baking time. **Serves 10 to 12.**

Bierocks

1 package hot roll mix
1 1/2 pounds ground beef
1 large onion, chopped
1 teaspoon salt
1/2 teaspoon pepper

1/2 teaspoon ground allspice
2 cups chopped cabbage
2 tablespoons all-purpose flour
1 tablespoon butter, melted

Prepare the dough using the roll mix package directions. Brown the ground beef in a skillet, stirring until crumbly; drain. Add the onion, salt, pepper and allspice. Cook until the onion is tender, stirring frequently. Stir in the cabbage and flour and cook for 2 minutes. Roll the dough into 20 thin 6-inch ovals on a lightly floured surface. Spoon equal portions of the cabbage mixture onto the center of each oval. Fold the dough to enclose the filling, sealing the edges. Arrange in a baking pan and brush with the butter. Bake at 350 degrees for 25 to 30 minutes or until brown. Serve with mustard. **Serves 20.**

Texas is the country's fifth-leading wine producing state. Wild grapes have always grown along rivers and streams in Texas, but it was not until the mid-1600s that they were cultivated. In the early 1900s, the wine industry thrived in Texas, until Prohibition wiped it out in 1919.

Soft Enchiladas

1 pound ground beef
1 pound hot bulk pork sausage
1 onion, chopped
Salt and pepper to taste
1 (10-ounce) can tomatoes with
    green chiles
1 teaspoon chili powder
$^1/_2$ teaspoon cumin seeds
$^1/_2$ teaspoon oregano
12 flour tortillas
1 (10-ounce) can condensed cream of
    chicken soup
8 ounces Velveeta cheese, cubed

Brown the ground beef and sausage with the onion in a skillet, stirring until crumbly; drain. Season with salt and pepper. Add the tomatoes with green chiles, chili powder, cumin seeds and oregano. Simmer, covered, for 5 minutes.

Spoon 3 to 4 tablespoonfuls of the mixture onto the center of each tortilla and fold to enclose the filling. Arrange in a 9×13-inch baking dish. Spread any remaining mixture over the enchiladas. Combine the soup and cheese in a saucepan over low heat. Cook until the cheese is melted, stirring constantly. Pour over the enchiladas. Bake at 350 degrees for 10 to 15 minutes or until hot and bubbly. **Serves 6.**

Marinated Pork Tenderloins with Mustard Horseradish Sauce

$1/2$ cup soy sauce

$1/2$ cup bourbon

$1/4$ cup packed brown sugar

2 (1-pound) pork tenderloins

$1/2$ cup sour cream

$1/2$ cup mayonnaise

1 tablespoon dry mustard

3 tablespoons prepared horseradish

1 tablespoon chopped scallions

1 garlic clove, minced

$1^1/2$ tablespoons white wine vinegar or
ginger and honey vinegar

Combine the soy sauce, bourbon and brown sugar in a bowl and mix
well. Pour into a 1-gallon sealable plastic bag. Add the pork, turning to
coat. Marinate in the refrigerator for 6 hours.

Combine the sour cream, mayonnaise, dry mustard, horseradish, scallions,
garlic and vinegar in a bowl and mix well. Chill, covered, for 4 hours or longer.

Place the pork in a baking pan. Pour the marinade over the pork. Bake
at 325 degrees for 1 hour or to 165 degrees on a meat thermometer, basting
frequently. Let stand, covered, for 15 minutes. Serve with the sour cream
mixture. *Serves 8.*

Meat will brown better if you blot off any excess moisture with a paper towel.

Pork Tenderloin with Honey Butter Sauce

$1/4$ cup ($1/2$ stick) butter
2 tablespoons honey
$1^1/2$ pounds pork tenderloin
Salt and pepper to taste
$1/4$ cup water

Heat the butter and honey in a Dutch oven over medium-low heat until the butter is melted, stirring to mix. Tuck the thin ends of the pork under and tie with kitchen string. Season the pork with salt and pepper and place in the Dutch oven. Cook for 15 minutes or until light brown on all sides, reducing the heat if the honey begins to burn.

Bake at 375 degrees for 15 to 30 minutes or to 145 degrees on a meat thermometer. Remove to a plate. Add the water to the pan drippings and mix well. Simmer over medium heat until reduced to $1/2$ cup, stirring and scraping up any browned bits. Slice the pork and drizzle with the sauce. **Serves 4.**

Chicken Parmesan

$1/2$ cup bread crumbs
$1/3$ cup grated Parmesan cheese
2 tablespoons parsley flakes
$1^1/2$ teaspoons salt
$3/4$ teaspoon pepper
$1/4$ cup ($1/2$ stick) margarine, melted
1 garlic clove, minced
2 teaspoons lemon juice
6 to 8 boneless skinless chicken breasts

Combine the bread crumbs, cheese, parsley, salt and pepper and mix well. Combine the margarine, garlic and lemon juice in a shallow dish and mix well. Dip the chicken into the margarine mixture and coat with the bread crumb mixture. Roll as for a jelly roll and place in a baking dish. Bake at 350 degrees for 1 hour or until cooked through. **Serves 6 to 8.**

Christmas Chicken Breasts with Corn Bread Dressing

1 cup all-purpose flour
1/4 cup sugar
4 teaspoons baking powder
3/4 teaspoon salt
1 cup yellow cornmeal
2 eggs
1 cup milk
1/4 cup vegetable shortening
1 cup chopped celery
1/4 cup chopped onion

1/2 cup (1 stick) margarine, melted
1/4 teaspoon sage
1/2 teaspoon salt
1/4 teaspoon pepper
1/2 cup chicken broth
4 eggs, hard-cooked and chopped
10 chicken breasts
Salt and pepper to taste
Butter

Combine the flour, sugar, baking powder, 3/4 teaspoon salt and the cornmeal in a bowl and mix well. Combine the eggs, milk and shortening in a bowl and mix well. Add the egg mixture to the flour mixture and whisk for 1 minute or just until smooth. Pour into a greased 9×9-inch baking pan. Bake at 425 degrees for 20 to 25 minutes. Let stand until cool.

Crumble the corn bread. Combine the celery, onion, margarine, sage, 1/2 teaspoon salt, 1/4 teaspoon pepper, the chicken broth, corn bread and eggs in a bowl and mix well. Drop by 1/2 cupfuls onto a foil-lined 10×15-inch baking pan, making 10 mounds. Season the chicken with salt and pepper to taste. Place a chicken breast skin side up on each mound, tucking edges under to form neat bundles. Brush the chicken with butter. Bake at 400 degrees for 25 minutes or until the chicken is brown and cooked through. *Serves 10.*

Asian Peanut Chicken

4 boneless skinless chicken breasts
1 teaspoon salt
1/2 teaspoon pepper
1/2 teaspoon garlic powder
1 1/2 tablespoons peanut oil
3/4 cup rice wine vinegar
1/2 teaspoon ground ginger
1 tablespoon sugar
1 teaspoon finely chopped fresh cilantro
3 tablespoons peanut butter
1 1/2 teaspoons soy sauce
2 tablespoons finely chopped peanuts
1 teaspoon finely chopped fresh cilantro

Season both sides of the chicken with the salt, pepper and garlic powder. Heat a skillet over medium-high heat. Add the peanut oil to the skillet. Cook the chicken in the oil for 3 to 4 minutes per side or until golden brown.

Combine the vinegar, ginger and sugar in a bowl and mix well. Pour over the chicken. Reduce the heat to medium. Cook, covered, for 8 to 10 minutes or until the chicken is cooked through. Remove the chicken to a serving plate; keep warm.

Add 1 teaspoon cilantro, the peanut butter and soy sauce to the pan drippings and mix well. Cook for 1 minute, stirring and scraping up any browned bits. Pour over the chicken. Sprinkle with the peanuts and 1 teaspoon cilantro. **Serves 4.**

Chicken with Lemon and Capers

4 to 6 boneless chicken breasts
Sea salt to taste
Cracked pepper to taste
3 to 4 tablespoons olive oil
3/4 cup white wine
2 tablespoons lemon juice

1 tablespoon grated lemon zest
2 tablespoons butter
1 tablespoon all-purpose flour
Cold water
3 to 4 tablespoons capers
Cream

Season the chicken with sea salt and pepper. Heat the olive oil in a skillet over medium heat until hot but not smoking. Cook the chicken in the hot oil for 3 to 4 minutes per side or until brown. Remove the chicken to a baking dish. Add the wine, lemon juice, lemon zest and butter to the pan drippings and mix well. Combine the flour with enough cold water to form a thin paste and mix well. Stir into the wine mixture. Stir in the capers and enough cream to make of the desired consistency. Pour 1/2 cup of the sauce over the chicken, keeping the remaining sauce warm. Bake, covered, at 325 degrees for 1 hour or until the chicken is cooked through. Pour the remaining sauce over the chicken and serve. ***Serves 4 to 6.***

> *Brining is a process of flavoring chicken or turkey in which the meat is soaked in a solution of sugar and salt so that it will hold its moisture and flavor. The salt brings out the proteins of the meat, while the sugar holds water and adds extra moisture to it.*

Peachy Chicken

1/2 cup all-purpose flour
1/2 teaspoon salt
1 teaspoon paprika
4 boneless skinless chicken breasts
2 tablespoons vegetable oil
1/2 cup dry sherry
2 tablespoons brown sugar

1 tablespoon soy sauce
1/2 teaspoon ground ginger
2 teaspoons sesame seeds
1 (16-ounce) can peach halves, drained
Hot cooked rice

Combine the flour, salt and paprika and mix well. Coat the chicken with the flour mixture. Cook the chicken in the oil in a skillet until brown on both sides; drain. Arrange the chicken in an 8×12-inch baking dish. Combine the sherry, brown sugar, soy sauce and ginger in a bowl and mix well. Pour over the chicken. Sprinkle with the sesame seeds. Bake, covered, at 350 degrees for 20 to 25 minutes. Add the peaches and bake for 20 minutes or until the chicken is cooked through and tender. Serve over rice. ***Serves 4.***

Chicken Marabella

1 (12-ounce) package pitted dried plums
1 (3-ounce) jar capers, drained
1 (1¹/2-ounce) bottle oregano
6 bay leaves
1 garlic bulb, minced
1 cup pimento-stuffed olives
¹/2 cup red wine vinegar
¹/2 cup olive oil
1 tablespoon coarse sea salt
2 teaspoons pepper
8 pounds chicken pieces
1 cup packed brown sugar
1 cup dry white wine
¹/4 cup chopped fresh parsley

Combine the dried plums, capers, oregano, bay leaves, garlic, olives, vinegar, olive oil, sea salt and pepper in a sealable plastic bag or bowl and mix well. Add the chicken, turning to coat. Chill for 8 hours or longer, turning occasionally. Arrange the chicken in a single layer in one or two 9×13-inch baking pans. Pour the marinade evenly over the chicken. Sprinkle with the brown sugar. Pour the wine around the chicken.

Bake at 350 degrees for 50 to 60 minutes or until the chicken is cooked through, basting frequently. Remove the chicken, dried plums, capers and olives to a serving plate, discarding the bay leaves. Drizzle with ³/4 cup of the pan drippings. Sprinkle the parsley evenly over the top. Serve with the remaining pan drippings. **Serves 10 to 12.**

The West Texas climate provides ideal conditions for growing grapes. Its warm sunny days, cool nights, low humidity, and sandy soil are similar to the wine regions of France.

Spicy Chicken Cacciatore

1 chicken, cut into 8 pieces
$1/4$ cup all-purpose flour
$1/4$ cup olive oil
1 large onion, chopped
2 garlic cloves, minced
$1^{1}/2$ cups sliced mushrooms
$1/2$ cup dry white wine
3 tablespoons tomato paste
$1/2$ cup dry white wine
1 small green bell pepper, chopped
2 cups chopped peeled tomatoes
1 bay leaf
$1/2$ teaspoon thyme
$1/4$ teaspoon basil
$1/8$ teaspoon marjoram
1 teaspoon salt
$1/4$ teaspoon pepper
3 tablespoons chopped fresh parsley
Grated Parmesan cheese

Coat the chicken with the flour. Cook in the olive oil in a skillet until brown on both sides. Remove to a plate using a slotted spoon. Cook the onion in the pan drippings until translucent, stirring frequently. Stir in the garlic. Cook until the onion is golden brown, stirring frequently. Stir in the mushrooms and $1/2$ cup wine, scraping up any browned bits. Stir in the tomato paste. Add $1/2$ cup wine, the bell pepper, tomatoes, bay leaf, thyme, basil, marjoram, salt, pepper and parsley and mix well. Return the chicken to the skillet and spoon the sauce over the chicken. Cook, covered, for 50 minutes or until the chicken is cooked through. Sprinkle with cheese. Serve with hot cooked pasta. You may bake the chicken mixture, covered, at 375 degrees for 50 minutes or bake, uncovered, for 15 minutes. *Serves 4.*

To toast a flour or corn tortilla, use tongs and hold the tortilla over a gas flame. Turn frequently to avoid burning.

Sour Cream Chicken Enchiladas

12 corn tortillas
Vegetable oil
4 boneless skinless chicken breasts, cooked, chopped and seasoned
4 cups (16 ounces) shredded Monterey Jack cheese
1 large onion, chopped

3 tablespoons margarine
1/4 cup all-purpose flour
1 cup chicken broth
1 can tomatoes with green chiles, drained
1 small can chopped green chiles, drained
1 cup sour cream

Coat the tortillas with a small amount of oil to soften. Spoon equal portions of the chicken, cheese and onion onto each tortilla, reserving a small amount of the cheese for the top. Roll to enclose the filling and place in a baking dish. Melt the margarine in a skillet. Add the flour and stir until the consistency of a paste. Add the chicken broth and cook until thickened, stirring constantly. Add the tomatoes with green chiles, green chiles and sour cream and mix well. Pour over the enchiladas. Sprinkle with the reserved cheese. Bake at 350 degrees for 20 to 30 minutes. **Serves 6.**

Poppy Seed Chicken

6 to 8 cups cooked rice
12 chicken breasts, cooked and chopped
2 cans condensed cream of chicken soup
3 cups sour cream

1/4 cup cooking sherry
2 tablespoons poppy seeds
Salt and pepper to taste
Butter cracker crumbs
6 tablespoons butter, melted

Layer the rice and chicken in a greased 9×13-inch baking pan. Combine the soup, sour cream, sherry, poppy seeds, salt and pepper in a bowl and mix well. Spoon evenly over the chicken. Sprinkle with butter cracker crumbs and drizzle with the butter. Bake at 350 degrees for 30 minutes or until hot and bubbly. **Serves 10 to 12.**

Chicken Curry

1 (2¹/₂-pound) chicken
2 tablespoons butter
2 onions, chopped
1 garlic clove, minced
2 tablespoons all-purpose flour
2 tablespoons curry powder
2 teaspoons ground ginger
2 teaspoons cardamom
2 tomatoes, chopped
1 apple, peeled and chopped
Salt to taste
Hot cooked rice

Combine the chicken and enough water to cover in a saucepan. Cook until the chicken is cooked through; drain, reserving and straining 2 cups of the broth. Chop the chicken, discarding the skin and bones. Melt the butter in a large saucepan. Sauté the onions and garlic in the hot butter until the onions are tender. Combine the flour, curry powder, ginger and cardamom and mix well. Stir into the onion mixture. Add the tomatoes, apple and reserved broth and mix well. Add the chicken and salt and cook, covered, for 1 hour. Serve over rice with chutney, peanuts, flaked coconut, chopped bananas and chopped cucumber. *Serves 8 to 10.*

Crawfish Etouffée

1 bunch green onions
$^1/_2$ cup (1 stick) butter
2 tablespoons vegetable oil
$^1/_2$ cup all-purpose flour
1 yellow onion, chopped
$^1/_2$ cup chopped celery
$^1/_2$ cup chopped fresh parsley
2 or 3 garlic cloves, minced
1 pound peeled crawfish tails
Salt and black pepper to taste
Cayenne pepper to taste
Chicken broth
4 or 5 cups hot cooked rice

Chop the green onions, reserving the tops. Melt the butter with the oil in a heavy skillet over medium heat. Add the flour and mix well. Cook the roux until light brown, stirring frequently. Add the chopped green onions, onion, celery, parsley and garlic. Cook until the onion is translucent, stirring constantly. Add the crawfish. Season with salt, black pepper and cayenne pepper. Stir in enough chicken broth to make of a thick soupy consistency. Cook, covered, over low heat for 15 minutes. Stir in the reserved green onion tops. Serve over the rice. ***Serves 4 or 5.***

Crawfish Fettuccini

1¹/2 cups (3 sticks) butter
3 onions, chopped
3 ribs celery, chopped
2 green bell peppers, chopped
¹/4 cup all-purpose flour
¹/4 cup chopped fresh parsley
3 pounds crawfish tails, peeled
4 cups half-and-half
1 pound Velveeta cheese, cubed
3 garlic cloves, crushed
Salt and pepper to taste
16 ounces fettuccini, cooked and drained
1 cup (4 ounces) grated Parmesan cheese (optional)

When selecting wine for a seafood dish, use the dominant flavor as a basis for determining your wine. A Texas chardonnay brings out a lemony flavor used in some seafood, and a pinot grigio also works well.

Melt the butter in a saucepan. Cook the onions, celery and bell peppers in the hot butter for 10 minutes or until the onions are translucent. Add the flour and mix well. Cook, covered, over medium-low heat for 15 minutes. Stir in the parsley and crawfish. Cook, covered, for 20 minutes. Add the half-and-half, Velveeta cheese and garlic and mix well. Season with salt and pepper. Cook over low heat for 20 minutes, stirring occasionally. Combine with the fettuccini in a bowl and mix well. Spoon into a 10×14-inch baking dish and sprinkle with the Parmesan cheese. Bake at 350 degrees for 12 to 15 minutes. **Serves 12.**

When shopping for seafood, look for shrimp and other types of seafood that have a clean, crisp scent with just a mild sea aroma. Avoid anything that has too strong an odor, especially of ammonia. Shrimp can be purchased raw and unshelled, shelled, or frozen. Uncooked shrimp may be kept refrigerated for two to three days or frozen for up to three months.

Shrimp with Feta Cheese

1 large onion, chopped
1/2 cup olive oil
1 (16-ounce) can diced tomatoes, drained
2 tablespoons chopped fresh cilantro
2 garlic cloves, minced
1 teaspoon salt
2 small dried red chiles, or 1/2 teaspoon cayenne pepper
2 pounds shrimp, peeled and deveined
8 ounces feta cheese, crumbled
1/4 cup vodka, heated (optional)

Sauté the onion in the olive oil in a skillet until translucent. Add the tomatoes, cilantro, garlic, salt and red chiles and mix well. Simmer, covered, for 1 hour. Add the shrimp and mix well. Pour into a 3-quart baking dish and sprinkle with the cheese. Bake at 350 for 10 to 15 minutes or until the shrimp turn pink. Remove the baking dish from the oven. Pour the vodka over the top and ignite. Serve after the flames recede. **Serves 4.**

Shrimp and Crab Meat au Gratin

1 cup finely chopped onion
1 rib celery, finely chopped
1/4 cup (1/2 stick) butter
1/2 cup all-purpose flour
1 (12-ounce) can evaporated milk
2 egg yolks
1 teaspoon salt
1/2 teaspoon cayenne pepper
3 tablespoons sherry
1 pound lump crab meat
1 pound shrimp, peeled and cooked
2 cups (8 ounces) shredded Cheddar cheese

Sauté the onion and celery in the butter in a skillet until tender. Stir in the flour. Add the evaporated milk gradually, stirring constantly. Add the egg yolks, salt, cayenne pepper and sherry and mix well. Cook for 5 minutes, stirring frequently. Pour over the crab meat and shrimp in a bowl and mix well. Spoon into a greased baking dish and sprinkle with the cheese. Bake at 375 degrees for 15 minutes; do not overbake. **Serves 6.**

Shrimp-Stuffed Eggplant

2 eggplant
¹/₂ cup chopped onion
¹/₂ cup chopped celery
¹/₄ cup (¹/₂ stick) margarine
4 garlic cloves, minced
2 hamburger buns, torn into
   small pieces

2 eggs, beaten
1 pound shrimp, peeled
   and boiled
Salt and pepper to taste
Chopped fresh parsley
   to taste

Cut the eggplant lengthwise into halves. Remove and chop the eggplant pulp, reserving the shells. Combine the eggplant pulp, onion, celery, margarine and garlic in a skillet and cook until tender, stirring frequently. Combine the hamburger buns and eggs in a bowl. Let stand until the eggs are absorbed. Combine with the eggplant mixture and shrimp in a bowl and mix well. Season with salt, pepper and parsley. Combine the eggplant shells and enough water to cover in a saucepan. Bring to a boil. Boil just until the eggplant shells are tender; drain. Spoon equal portions of the shrimp mixture into each eggplant shell and arrange in a baking dish. Bake at 350 degrees for 15 minutes. **Serves 4.**

Shrimp Scampi

¹/₂ cup (1 stick) butter
2 teaspoons Worcestershire sauce
¹/₄ cup sherry
1 garlic clove, crushed
2 tablespoons lemon juice
1 tablespoon sugar

1 pound shrimp, peeled and
   deveined
¹/₄ cup minced fresh parsley
2 cups cooked rice
Grated Parmesan cheese

Melt the butter in a skillet over low heat. Add the Worcestershire sauce, sherry, garlic, lemon juice and sugar and mix well. Spoon over the shrimp in an 11×13-inch baking dish. Broil under low heat for 8 minutes. Let stand for 15 minutes. Sprinkle with the parsley. Broil under high heat for 3 minutes. Spoon over the rice in a serving dish and sprinkle with cheese. You may cook the rice with green onion tops in chicken broth. **Serves 2 to 4.**

Shrimp Etouffée

1/4 cup (1/2 stick) margarine
2 tablespoons all-purpose flour
1 1/2 cups chopped celery
1 cup chopped green bell pepper
1 cup chopped onion
1 1/2 teaspoons minced garlic
1/2 cup vegetable juice cocktail
1/2 cup condensed cream of celery soup
1/2 teaspoon salt
1/2 teaspoon cayenne pepper
1/8 teaspoon hot red pepper sauce, or to taste
1 pound small to medium shelled, deveined and cooked shrimp
Hot cooked rice

Melt the margarine in a Dutch oven or cast-iron saucepan. Stir in the flour. Cook until light brown, stirring constantly. Add the celery, bell pepper, onion and garlic. Cook until tender, stirring frequently. Add the vegetable juice cocktail, soup, salt, cayenne pepper and hot sauce and mix well. Cook for 15 to 20 minutes, stirring frequently. Add the shrimp. Cook for 15 to 20 minutes or until the shrimp turn pink, stirring frequently to prevent sticking and adding additional vegetable juice cocktail if needed to make of the desired consistency. Serve over rice. **Serves 4 to 5.**

Shrimp Jambalaya

1/2 cup vegetable oil
3 ribs celery, chopped
1 onion, chopped
2 cups rice
3 cans chicken broth
3 chicken broth cans water
30 ounces tomato sauce
30 ounces water
1 teaspoon liquid shrimp and crab boil
1 teaspoon thyme
4 teaspoons parsley flakes
Salt and pepper to taste
3 pounds shrimp, peeled

Heat the oil in a Dutch oven. Add the celery, onion and rice and cook until the rice is dark brown and the celery and onion are tender, stirring frequently. Add the chicken broth, 3 cans water, tomato sauce, 30 ounces water, shrimp and crab boil, thyme, parsley, salt and pepper and mix well. Cook, covered, for 25 minutes or until the rice is tender. Add the shrimp and cook for 5 minutes or until the shrimp turn pink. **Serves 10 to 12.**

To clarify butter, place it in a glass loaf pan and melt it slowly in an oven or microwave to separate the milk solids. Once melted, cover and chill for several hours. Once chilled, scrape off the white solids and discard. Using a knife, poke holes in the butter, making sure to go all the way to the bottom of the pan. Holding the butter in place, tip the dish to discard the remaining milky liquid. The solid butter that remains is clarified butter, which does not burn as easily since the milk solids have been removed.

126

Baked Cherry Perch

4 cherry perch fillets
1 cup sour cream
1/2 cup (2 ounces) grated Parmesan cheese
1/2 teaspoon paprika
1/4 teaspoon pepper
2 tablespoons Italian-style bread crumbs
3 tablespoons butter, melted

Place the fish in a greased baking dish. Combine the sour cream, cheese, paprika and pepper in a bowl and mix well. Spread over the fish. Sprinkle with the bread crumbs and drizzle with the butter. Bake at 350 degrees for 25 minutes. **Serves 4.**

Grilled Orange and Bourbon Salmon

1/4 cup bourbon
1/4 cup fresh orange juice
1/4 cup low-sodium soy sauce
1/4 cup packed brown sugar
1/4 cup chopped green onions
3 tablespoons chopped fresh chives
2 tablespoons fresh lemon juice
2 garlic cloves, minced
4 (6-ounce) salmon fillets (about 1 inch thick)

Combine the bourbon, orange juice, soy sauce, brown sugar, green onions, chives, lemon juice and garlic in a sealable plastic bag. Add the fish. Marinate in the refrigerator for 1 1/2 hours, turning the bag occasionally. Remove the fish from the marinade, reserving the marinade. Grill the fish for 6 minutes per side or until the fish flakes easily, basting frequently with the reserved marinade. **Serves 4.**

Red Snapper Veracruz

1 (28-ounce) can diced tomatoes
1/4 cup extra-virgin olive oil
1/4 cup finely chopped onion
3 large garlic cloves, chopped
3 small bay leaves
2 tablespoons chopped fresh parsley
1 teaspoon Mexican oregano
1/4 cup chopped green olives
2 tablespoons raisins (optional)
2 tablespoons drained capers
Salt and pepper to taste
6 (4- to 5-ounce) red snapper fillets

Drain the tomatoes, reserving the juice. Crush the tomatoes in a bowl using a potato masher until coarsely puréed. Drain, reserving the juice. Heat the olive oil in a heavy skillet over medium-high heat. Sauté the onion and garlic in the hot oil under tender. Add the tomato purée and cook for 3 minutes. Add the bay leaves, parsley, oregano and 1/4 cup of the reserved tomato juice. Simmer for 3 minutes or until thickened, stirring occasionally. Add the olives, raisins, capers and the remaining reserved tomato juice. Simmer for 10 minutes or until thickened, stirring occasionally. Season with salt and pepper. Spread 5 tablespoons of the sauce over the bottom of a 10×15-inch glass baking dish. Arrange the fish on top of the sauce. Sprinkle lightly with salt and pepper. Spoon the remaining sauce over the fish. Bake at 425 degrees for 20 minutes or until the fish is opaque. Remove to serving plates. Garnish with pickled jalapeño chile halves, cilantro sprigs and avocado slices. **Serves 6.**

Greek Fish

1 1/2 pounds fish fillets
  (such as tilapia)
1 1/2 teaspoon salt
1/2 teaspoon paprika
1/2 teaspoon lemon pepper
1 green bell pepper, cut into rings
1 tomato, sliced

1 small onion, sliced
1 cup mushrooms
2 tablespoons lemon juice
2 tablespoons olive oil
2 or 3 garlic cloves, chopped
1 tablespoon soy sauce

Arrange the fish in an 8×8-inch baking dish. Sprinkle with the salt, paprika and lemon pepper. Arrange the bell pepper, tomato, onion and mushrooms on top of the fish. Combine the lemon juice, olive oil, garlic and soy sauce in a bowl and mix well. Pour over the fish and vegetables. Bake, covered, at 375 degrees for 10 minutes. Bake, uncovered, for 15 minutes or until the fish flakes easily. You may serve the fish over rice. **Serves 4.**

Baked Birds

20 birds (such as quail or dove)
1/2 cup all-purpose flour
1/2 cup baking mix
Butter
1 (8-ounce) package mushrooms

1 small onion, chopped
1/2 cup sherry
1 can condensed cream of
  mushroom soup
1 cup heavy cream

Clean the birds. Combine the flour and baking mix and mix well. Coat the birds with the flour mixture. Melt a small amount of butter in an ovenproof skillet. Brown the birds in the hot butter. Remove the birds to a plate using a slotted spoon. Sauté the mushrooms and onion in the drippings. Stir in the sherry and soup. Return the birds to the skillet. Bake at 325 degrees for 45 minutes or until cooked through. Add the cream to the skillet and bake for 15 minutes. You may serve the birds over rice. **Serves 4.**

Pasta with Prosciutto Sauce

1 pound ground beef
2 onions, sliced
2 garlic cloves, finely chopped
1 (28-ounce) can tomatoes
8 ounces prosciutto or dried beef,
    cut into thin strips
3/4 cup dry red wine
1 teaspoon sugar
1/2 teaspoon salt
1/2 teaspoon rosemary, crushed
1/4 teaspoon nutmeg
1/4 teaspoon pepper
16 ounces mostaccioli or ziti
Freshly grated Parmesan cheese or
    Romano cheese

Brown the ground beef with the onions and garlic in a 10-inch skillet, stirring until crumbly; drain. Stir in the undrained tomatoes, prosciutto, wine, sugar, salt, rosemary, nutmeg and pepper, chopping the tomatoes with a fork. Simmer, covered, for 15 minutes, stirring occasionally. Simmer, uncovered, for 1 hour. Cook the mostaccioli using the package directions; drain. Serve the sauce over the pasta. Sprinkle with cheese. **Serves 8.**

Angel Hair Pasta with Pesto Cream Sauce

12 ounces angel hair pasta
2 to 3 tablespoons olive oil
4 boneless skinless chicken
   breasts, chopped
1 cup mushrooms, sliced

1 cup heavy cream
1 cup (2 sticks) butter
3/4 cup (3 ounces) grated
   Parmesan cheese
1/4 cup pesto

The key to good Parmesan cheese is the amount of time it has been aged. If it is aged for eighteen months or longer, it will have tiny crystal shards that crunch when eaten. These crystal shards are a protein that develops during the aging process.

Cook the angel hair pasta using the package directions; drain. Heat the olive oil in a skillet. Sauté the chicken in the hot oil until cooked through. Remove to a plate; drain the skillet. Sauté the mushrooms in the skillet until tender, adding additional oil if needed. Heat the cream in a saucepan. Add the butter and cook until the butter is melted, stirring frequently. Stir in the cheese. Reduce the heat to low. Add the pesto and mix well. Add the chicken and mushrooms and mix well. Serve over the pasta. ***Serves 6.***

Broccoli Manicotti

6 ounces ground turkey or
   chicken (optional)
1 egg, beaten
1 cup ricotta cheese
1 cup cottage cheese
2 cups (8 ounces) shredded
   mozzarella cheese

1/2 teaspoon thyme (optional)
1 cup chopped broccoli
1/4 cup chopped onion
8 ounces manicotti
1 jar spaghetti sauce
Grated Parmesan cheese

Brown the ground turkey in a skillet, stirring until crumbly; drain. Remove to a bowl. Add the egg, ricotta cheese, cottage cheese, mozzarella cheese and thyme and mix well. Stir in the broccoli and onion. Fill the uncooked manicotti with the broccoli mixture. Arrange in a baking dish. Pour the spaghetti sauce over the manicotti; cover with foil. Bake at 375 degrees for 30 minutes. Bake, uncovered, for 20 to 30 minutes or until the manicotti is tender. Sprinkle with Parmesan cheese. You may prepare the manicotti a day ahead and chill, covered, until baking time. ***Serves 6.***

Fettuccini Primavera

9 ounces refrigerated fettuccini
3/4 cup water
1 cup broccoli florets
1/2 cup sliced carrots
1/2 cup red bell pepper strips
3 tablespoons butter or margarine
2 tablespoons all-purpose flour
1 cup evaporated milk
1/2 cup chicken broth
1/2 cup (2 ounces) grated Parmesan cheese
1/2 cup (2 ounces) grated provolone cheese
1/8 teaspoon cayenne pepper
Freshly ground black pepper to taste

Cook the fettuccini using the package directions; drain. Bring 3/4 cup water to a boil in a saucepan. Add the broccoli, carrots and bell pepper. Reduce the heat. Simmer for 5 to 7 minutes; drain. Melt the butter in a saucepan. Stir in the flour. Add the evaporated milk and chicken broth gradually, stirring constantly. Cook until boiling and thickened, stirring constantly. Add the Parmesan cheese, provolone cheese, cayenne pepper and black pepper and cook until the cheese is melted, stirring constantly. Combine with the fettuccini in a serving dish and toss to coat. Add the vegetables and stir to coat. You may substitute 16 ounces frozen vegetables for the broccoli, carrots and bell pepper; cook using the package directions before proceeding. You may substitute 8 ounces dry fettuccini for the refrigerated fettuccini; cook using the package directions. You may add 1 cup chopped cooked chicken or shrimp. **Serves 4.**

Southwestern Summer Pasta

3 small tomatoes
2 tablespoons extra-virgin olive oil
3 garlic cloves, minced
1 jalapeño chile, seeded and finely chopped
3 tablespoons chopped fresh cilantro
1 tablespoon fresh lime juice
$1/2$ teaspoon chili powder
$1/4$ teaspoon salt
$1/4$ teaspoon white pepper
4 ounces fresh angel hair pasta or spaghetti
4 ounces goat cheese, crumbled
2 tablespoons pine nuts, toasted

Chop the tomatoes coarsely into a bowl, retaining the juices. Add the olive oil, garlic, jalapeño chile, cilantro, lime juice, chili powder, salt and white pepper and mix well. Let stand, covered, for 1 hour. Cook the angel hair pasta using the package directions; drain. Serve the tomato mixture over the pasta. Top with the cheese and pine nuts. Serve with crusty bread. **Serves 2.**

Penne with Vodka Cream Sauce

2 tablespoons olive oil
1 large onion, finely chopped
3 tablespoons minced garlic
1 (28-ounce) can crushed tomatoes
1/4 cup vodka
1/4 teaspoon red pepper flakes
2 cups heavy cream
1/4 cup chopped fresh basil
Salt and pepper to taste
1 pound penne, cooked al dente
  and drained

Heat the olive oil in a skillet over medium heat. Sauté the onion in
the hot oil for 5 minutes. Add the garlic and cook for 1 minute, stirring
constantly. Stir in the tomatoes, vodka and red pepper flakes. Simmer for
10 minutes. Stir in the cream, basil, salt and pepper. Serve over the penne.
Serves 6.

One-Dish Wonders

Casseroles and Quick Dishes
for People on the Go

Coastal Living

Photograph courtesy of Ann McDonald

*A casserole is an easy dish to take to the beach
for a family outing. Take plenty of pillows and
a huge blanket so that everyone can sit together
and eat comfortably. Place candles in glass jars
filled with sand and shells for the late-night
beachcombers.*

Beef Stew Burgundy

1 pound (1-inch) beef cubes
1 package frozen stew vegetables
1 can condensed tomato soup
1 can diced tomatoes or
    seasoned diced tomatoes
1 can black beans
2 tablespoons brown sugar
1/4 cup Worcestershire sauce
2 tablespoons soy sauce
3/4 cup red wine
Salt and pepper to taste
1 cup (about) water

This is an easy way to let the oven or slow cooker do all of the work. Add leftover vegetables, such as green beans, corn, potatoes, or onions. Use leftover wine that has been opened, or omit the wine and add more water or broth.

Combine the beef, vegetables, soup, tomatoes, undrained black beans, brown sugar, Worcestershire sauce, soy sauce, wine, salt and pepper in a bowl and mix well. Stir in enough of the water to make of a thick but not stiff consistency. Pour into a 3 1/2-quart baking dish. Bake, covered, at 250 degrees for 5 hours or until the beef is cooked through and tender, adding additional water or wine if needed. You may cook the stew in a slow cooker, covered, for 8 hours. **Serves 4 to 6.**

Slow-Cooker Beef Stroganoff

2 pounds (1-inch) beef cubes
1 large onion, chopped (about 1 cup)
1 (10-ounce) can condensed golden mushroom soup
1 (10-ounce) can condensed cream of onion soup
1 (8-ounce) can sliced mushrooms, drained
1/4 teaspoon pepper
8 ounces cream cheese, chopped
1 cup sour cream
6 cups hot cooked noodles

Combine the beef, onion, golden mushroom soup, cream of onion soup, mushrooms and pepper in a slow cooker. Cook, covered, on Low for 8 to 10 hours or until the beef is cooked through and very tender. Add the cream cheese and cook until melted, stirring constantly. Stir in the sour cream. Serve over the noodles. *Serves 8.*

Lasagna Italiana

1 pound ground beef
3/4 cup chopped onion
2 tablespoons vegetable oil
1 (16-ounce) can tomatoes, chopped
2 cans tomato paste
2 cups water
1 tablespoon chopped fresh parsley
2 teaspoons salt
1 teaspoon sugar
1 teaspoon garlic powder
1/2 teaspoon pepper
1/2 teaspoon oregano
12 lasagna noodles
16 ounces cottage cheese or ricotta cheese
3 cups (12 ounces) shredded mozzarella cheese

Brown the ground beef with the onion in the oil in a skillet, stirring until crumbly; drain. Add the tomatoes, tomato paste, water, parsley, salt, sugar, garlic powder, pepper and oregano and mix well. Simmer for 30 minutes, stirring occasionally. Cook the noodles using the package directions; drain. Spread 1 cup of the sauce over the bottom of a 9×13-inch baking pan. Layer 1/3 at a time with the noodles, cottage cheese, remaining sauce and mozzarella cheese, ending with the sauce and mozzarella cheese. Bake at 350 degrees for 45 minutes. *Serves 10 to 12.*

Famous Beef Lasagna

1¹/₂ pounds ground beef
¹/₂ onion, chopped
1 green bell pepper, chopped
1 can diced tomatoes
1 can diced Italian-style tomatoes or
   garlic and onion tomatoes
1 (8-ounce) can tomato sauce
1 package lasagna noodles
8 ounces cottage cheese
4 ounces cream cheese, softened
2 eggs
8 slices mozzarella cheese
2 cups (8 ounces) shredded mozzarella cheese

Brown the ground beef with the onion and bell pepper in a skillet, stirring until crumbly; drain. Add the diced tomatoes, Italian-style tomatoes and tomato sauce and mix well. Cook for 30 minutes or longer, stirring frequently. Cook the noodles using the package directions; drain. Combine the cottage cheese, cream cheese and eggs in a bowl and mix with a fork.

Layer the noodles, sliced mozzarella cheese, cottage cheese mixture and ground beef mixture ¹/₂ at a time in a 10×13-inch baking pan, ending with the ground beef mixture. Sprinkle with ¹/₂ of the shredded mozzarella cheese. Bake, covered with foil, at 350 degrees for 1 hour. Sprinkle with the remaining shredded mozzarella cheese. Bake, uncovered, for 10 minutes or until the cheese is melted and bubbly. *Serves 12.*

Spaghetti Supreme

1¹/2 pounds ground beef

1¹/2 cups chopped onions

1 cup chopped green bell pepper

¹/2 cup chopped celery

2 garlic cloves, crushed

1 (10-ounce) can low-fat condensed
    cream of mushroom soup

³/4 cup water

1 (14-ounce) can tomatoes, chopped

2 tablespoons chili powder

¹/4 teaspoon salt

¹/4 teaspoon pepper

8 ounces spaghetti

2 ounces Cheddar cheese, cut into ¹/2-inch cubes

2 tablespoons chopped pimento-stuffed olives

¹/2 cup (2 ounces) shredded Cheddar cheese

Brown the ground beef with the onions, bell pepper, celery and garlic in a
Dutch oven, stirring until crumbly; drain. Stir in the soup, water, undrained
tomatoes, chili powder, salt and pepper. Bring to a boil over medium heat.
Simmer for 1 hour, stirring occasionally.

Cook the spaghetti using the package directions; drain. Stir the spaghetti,
cheese cubes and olives into the ground beef mixture. Spoon into a baking
dish sprayed with nonstick cooking spray. Bake, covered, at 325 degrees for
20 minutes or until heated through. Sprinkle with the shredded cheese.
Bake, uncovered, for 10 minutes. **Serves 8.**

Chicken Enchilada Casserole

1 large chicken, cooked and chopped
1 (10-ounce) can condensed cream of mushroom soup
1 (10-ounce) can condensed cream of chicken soup
1 (10-ounce) can condensed cream of celery soup
1 garlic clove, minced
1 small can chopped green chiles
1 package corn tortillas
4 cups (16 ounces) shredded mild Cheddar cheese
Chopped lettuce
Chopped tomatoes
Sour cream (optional)

Combine the chicken, cream of mushroom soup, cream of chicken soup, cream of celery soup, garlic and green chiles in a saucepan and mix well. Cook for 10 minutes, stirring frequently. Add the tortillas to the mixture. Let stand just until the tortillas are softened. Arrange a single layer of tortillas in a 9×13-inch baking dish sprayed with nonstick cooking spray, overlapping as needed. Layer with 1/3 of the chicken mixture and 1/3 of the cheese. Repeat the layers of tortillas, chicken mixture and cheese until all of the ingredients are used, ending with the cheese. Bake, covered, at 350 degrees for 30 minutes. Top with lettuce, tomatoes and sour cream just before serving. **Serves 10 to 12.**

Favorite Mexican Chicken Casserole

1 (10-ounce) can condensed
   cream of mushroom soup
$2/3$ cup milk
$1/2$ teaspoon salt
1 cup cottage cheese
8 ounces cream cheese
3 cups chopped cooked chicken
$1/2$ teaspoon poultry seasoning
$1/3$ cup chopped onion
1 (4-ounce) can chopped green chiles
Tabasco sauce to taste
1 package tortilla chips
2 cups (8 ounces) shredded Cheddar cheese
Grated Parmesan cheese
Bread crumbs

The corn or flour tortilla is a staple in Mexican cooking and is sometimes served in place of bread. Tortillas will keep for up to two months if stored in plastic in the refrigerator. To heat, place them in a dry skillet over medium-high heat until warm, turning once to heat both sides. They can also be warmed in the microwave by placing them in a damp towel.

Combine the soup, milk and salt in a saucepan and cook until heated through. Stir in the cottage cheese and cream cheese. Cook until the cream cheese is melted, stirring occasionally. Add the chicken, poultry seasoning, onion, green chiles and Tabasco sauce. Cook until heated through, stirring occasionally. Layer the tortilla chips, chicken mixture and Cheddar cheese in a 2-quart baking dish. Sprinkle with Parmesan cheese and bread crumbs. Bake at 350 degrees for 30 minutes. You may freeze the casserole before baking and adjust the baking time. ***Serves 4 to 6.***

Crunchy Chicken Casserole

Although it is becoming more and more popular as a convenient cooking method, the casserole is actually an old method of food preparation. It takes its name from the primitive pieces of shallow pottery that were called "casseroles."

5$^{1}/_{2}$ cups chopped cooked chicken
3 cups chopped celery
1 cup slivered almonds
3 tablespoons grated onion
1 or 2 (8-ounce) cans sliced water chestnuts
   (optional)
1 teaspoon salt
1 teaspoon poultry seasoning
Pepper to taste
1$^{1}/_{2}$ cups mayonnaise
$^{1}/_{4}$ cup lemon juice
1 cup (4 ounces) shredded Cheddar cheese
Crushed potato chips

Combine the chicken, celery, almonds, onion, water chestnuts, salt, poultry seasoning, pepper, mayonnaise and lemon juice in a bowl and mix well. Spoon into a buttered 9×13-inch baking dish. Sprinkle with the cheese and potato chips. Bake at 350 degrees for 30 minutes. ***Serves 12 to 14.***

Chicken Lasagna

3 cups shredded cooked chicken

1 cup sour cream

2 (10-ounce) cans condensed cream of chicken or cream of
mushroom soup

1 (4-ounce) can mushrooms, drained

4 cups (16 ounces) shredded Monterey Jack cheese

1 (10-ounce) package frozen chopped spinach, cooked

1 package lasagna noodles, cooked and drained

Combine the chicken, sour cream, soup, mushrooms, cheese and spinach
in a bowl and mix well. Place 2 layers of the noodles in a greased 9×13-inch
baking pan. Spread 1/3 of the chicken mixture over the noodles. Repeat
the layers of noodles and chicken mixture until all of the ingredients are
used, ending with the chicken mixture. Bake, covered, at 350 degrees for
30 minutes. Bake, uncovered, for 15 minutes. You may sprinkle the top
of the lasagna with additional cheese before baking, substitute ground
turkey for the chicken and/or freeze individual servings for future use.
Serves 10 to 12.

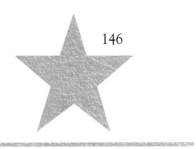

Chicken Tetrazzini

5 to 6 pounds chicken, cut up
Salt and pepper to taste
16 ounces thin spaghetti
1/2 cup (1 stick) margarine
1 large green bell pepper, chopped
2 (3-ounce) cans chopped mushrooms
1/4 cup chopped pimentos
1 teaspoon salt
1/4 teaspoon pepper
1 tablespoon Worcestershire sauce
3 tablespoons all-purpose flour
1/2 cup cooking sherry
2 cups milk, at room temperature
2 (10-ounce) cans condensed cream of mushroom soup
1/4 teaspoon garlic powder
3 cups (12 ounces) shredded American cheese
1 cup (4 ounces) grated Parmesan cheese
Shredded American cheese

Combine the chicken and enough water to cover in a large saucepan. Season with salt and pepper to taste. Bring to a boil. Cook until cooked through; drain, reserving the broth. Let stand until cool. Cut the chicken into bite-size pieces, discarding the skin and bones. Reserve 1 cup of the broth. Cook the spaghetti in the remaining broth using the package directions; drain. Melt the margarine in a saucepan over medium heat. Sauté the bell pepper in the hot margarine until tender. Add the mushrooms, pimentos, 1 teaspoon salt and 1/4 teaspoon pepper and mix well. Stir in the Worcestershire sauce. Cook until dark brown, stirring frequently. Stir in the flour, sherry, milk, soup and garlic powder. Add the chicken, reserved broth, 3 cups American cheese and the Parmesan cheese. Cook until the cheese is melted, stirring constantly. Combine the chicken mixture and spaghetti in a bowl and mix well. Spoon into 2 buttered 9×13-inch baking dishes. Sprinkle with a small amount of American cheese. Bake at 350 degrees for 30 minutes or until bubbly. *Serves 8 to 10.*

Chicken Continental

1 jar dried beef
6 boneless skinless chicken breasts
6 slices bacon
1 (10-ounce) can condensed cream of mushroom soup
$1/2$ cup sour cream
$1/4$ cup all-purpose flour
Hot cooked rice or egg noodles

Line the bottom and side of a slower cooker with the dried beef. Wrap the chicken with the bacon and place in the slow cooker. Combine the soup, sour cream and flour in a bowl and mix well. Pour the soup mixture over the chicken. Cook, covered, on Low for 8 to 10 hours or on High for 4 to 6 hours. Serve over rice. You may substitute chicken tenders for the chicken breasts and/or use fat-free or low-fat soup and sour cream. **Serves 6.**

Lemon Cornish Hens

1 lemon, cut into 6 or 9 slices
3 (22-ounce) frozen Cornish game hens, thawed
4 garlic cloves, minced
4 teaspoons minced fresh thyme
Juice of 1 lemon
2 tablespoons butter, melted
$1/2$ teaspoon salt
$1/2$ teaspoon freshly ground pepper
$1/2$ cup sliced almonds, toasted
1 lemon, sliced

Place 2 or 3 slices of 1 lemon in each hen cavity. Place 1 of the minced garlic cloves and 1 teaspoon of the minced thyme in each cavity. Place the hens in a slow cooker. Combine the juice of 1 lemon, the butter, remaining garlic, remaining thyme, salt and pepper in a bowl and mix well. Drizzle over the hens. Sprinkle with $1/4$ cup of the sliced almonds. Cook, covered, on Low for 8 to 10 hours or on High for 4 to 6 hours. Arrange the hens on a serving plate. Sprinkle with the remaining $1/4$ cup almonds and serve with the remaining lemon slices. Garnish with thyme sprigs. You may cut the hens into halves to serve 6 people. **Serves 3.**

Shrimp and Wild Rice Casserole

*Deveining shrimp is a
matter of personal preference.
Generally, small and medium
shrimp do not need deveining
except for cosmetic purposes.
However, the veins of larger
shrimp should usually
be removed.*

1/4 cup (1/2 cup) butter
4 green onions with tops, chopped
1 garlic clove
1 small green bell pepper, chopped
2 packages long grain and wild rice
2 pounds shrimp, cooked, shelled and deveined
2 (10-ounce) cans condensed cream of chicken soup
1 cup mayonnaise
1 small jar chopped pimento
1 (16-ounce) can green beans, drained
1 (5-ounce) can water chestnuts, drained and sliced
1 cup (4 ounces) shredded Monterey Jack cheese
1 cup (4 ounces) shredded Cheddar cheese
1/2 cup (2 ounces) grated Parmesan cheese
Dash of Tabasco sauce
Dash of Worcestershire sauce
Salt and pepper to taste
1 cup buttered bread crumbs

Melt the butter in a saucepan. Sauté the green onions, garlic and bell
pepper in the hot butter until tender. Cook the rice using the package
directions. Combine the shrimp, rice, soup, mayonnaise, pimento, green
beans, water chestnuts, Monterey Jack cheese, Cheddar cheese, Parmesan
cheese, Tabasco sauce, Worcestershire sauce, salt and pepper in a bowl and
mix well. Spoon into a greased 9×13-inch baking dish. Top with the bread
crumbs. Bake at 350 degrees for 30 minutes. This casserole freezes well.
Serves 12.

Spinach and Artichoke Casserole

2 (10-ounce) packages frozen chopped spinach,
   thawed and squeezed dry
1 (13-ounce) can artichoke hearts,
   drained and chopped
$1/2$ cup heavy cream
$1/8$ teaspoon salt
$1/8$ teaspoon coarsely ground pepper
$1/2$ cup (2 ounces) grated Parmesan cheese
8 ounces cream cheese, softened
1 cup milk
$1/3$ cup grated Parmesan cheese

Combine the spinach, artichokes, cream, salt, pepper and $1/2$ cup Parmesan cheese in a bowl and mix well. Place the cream cheese in a mixing bowl and beat at medium speed until fluffy, scraping the bowl occasionally using a rubber spatula. Add the milk gradually, beating constantly at low speed just until blended. Spoon the spinach mixture into a shallow $1^1/2$-quart or 8×8-inch glass baking dish. Pour the cream cheese mixture evenly over the spinach mixture. Sprinkle with $1/3$ cup Parmesan cheese. Bake at 350 degrees for 45 to 55 minutes or until the edges are bubbly and the top is golden brown. **Serves 6.**

On the Side

Vegetables, Side Dishes and Breads

Party on the Patio

Photograph courtesy of Chelsie Murphy

Line the bottom and sides of a glass vase with apple wedges and lemon or lime slices, then add fresh flowers. The fruit will enhance the appearance of the arrangement as well as feed the flowers. The lemons keep the apples and other fruit from turning brown.

If an outdoor party extends into the evening hours, candles on the table or simple spotlights shining on the table can set the mood and help guests to see.

Italian Artichoke Casserole

8 ounces mushrooms, sliced
1 cup olive oil
2 (10-ounce) packages frozen artichoke hearts, partially thawed
1 tablespoon Italian seasoning
2 cups bread crumbs
1 garlic clove, minced
1/2 teaspoon fresh mint leaves, finely chopped
1 cup (4 ounces) freshly grated Parmesan cheese

Sauté the mushrooms in 1 tablespoon of the olive oil in a skillet until tender. Add the remaining olive oil, artichokes and Italian seasoning and mix well. Let stand, covered, for 1 hour. Combine the bread crumbs, garlic, mint and cheese in a bowl and mix well. Add to the artichoke mixture and mix well. Pour into an 8×8-inch baking dish. Bake at 375 degrees for 50 to 60 minutes or until brown and bubbly. You may substitute fresh or canned artichoke hearts for the frozen artichoke hearts. **Serves 8.**

Artichoke Hearts and Brussels Sprouts

2/3 cup mayonnaise
2 tablespoons lemon juice
1/4 cup (1/2 stick) butter, melted
1/4 cup grated Parmesan cheese
1 package brussels sprouts, cooked and drained
1 can artichoke hearts, drained and cut into quarters
1/4 cup slivered almonds

Combine the mayonnaise, lemon juice, butter and cheese in a bowl and mix well. Layer the brussels sprouts and artichokes in a buttered baking dish. Spoon the mayonnaise mixture over the top. Sprinkle with the almonds. Bake at 400 degrees for 8 to 10 minutes or until light brown and bubbly. You may double or triple the recipe. **Serves 6.**

Green Beans Ro-Tel

2 (14-ounce) cans French-style green beans, drained
1/2 (10-ounce) can Ro-Tel tomatoes with green chiles
2 tablespoons margarine
1 1/2 tablespoons all-purpose flour
1/2 cup milk
4 ounces Velveeta cheese
Salt and pepper to taste

Combine the green beans and tomatoes with green chiles in a slow cooker and mix well. Melt the margarine in a saucepan. Stir in the flour until smooth. Add the milk gradually, stirring constantly. Add the cheese and cook over low heat until melted, stirring constantly. Season with salt and pepper. Pour over the green bean mixture and mix well. Cook, covered, on High until bubbly. You may bake the green bean mixture at 375 degrees in a 2-quart baking dish for 20 minutes or until bubbly. **Serves 6.**

Broccoli and Cheese

1 onion, chopped
1/2 cup (1 stick) butter
1 (2-ounce) roll garlic cheese
1 (10-ounce) can condensed cream of mushroom soup
1 (10-ounce) can chopped mushrooms
1/2 cup slivered almonds
2 (10-ounce) packages frozen broccoli spears

Sauté the onion in the butter in a skillet until tender. Add the cheese and cook until melted, stirring constantly. Add the soup, mushrooms and almonds and mix well. Cook the broccoli using the package directions; drain. Layer the broccoli and the cheese mixture alternately in a baking dish. Bake at 350 degrees for 15 to 20 minutes or until bubbly. **Serves 6 to 8.**

Carrot Puff

16 ounces carrots
$1/2$ cup (1 stick) butter, melted
3 eggs
1 teaspoon vanilla extract
1 cup sugar
3 tablespoons all-purpose flour
1 teaspoon baking powder

Peel the carrots and cut into 1-inch pieces. Bring enough water to cover the carrots to a boil in a saucepan. Add the carrots and cook until tender; drain. Combine the butter, eggs, vanilla, sugar, flour and baking powder in a blender and process until mixed. Add the carrots a few at a time, processing constantly until puréed. Pour into a greased 8×8-inch baking dish. Bake at 350 degrees for 45 minutes or until set. You may prepare the carrot mixture ahead of time and chill, covered, until ready to bake. Bring to room temperature before baking. **Serves 6 to 8.**

Frosted Cauliflower

1 (2-pound) head cauliflower
Salt and pepper to taste
$1/2$ cup mayonnaise
2 teaspoons prepared mustard
$1/4$ teaspoon salt
1 cup (4 ounces) or more shredded Cheddar cheese

Remove the tough base of the cauliflower, leaving the head intact. Pierce the remaining base of the cauliflower all over with a knife. Place the cauliflower head side up in a baking dish. Microwave, covered, on High for 10 to 12 minutes or until tender. Let stand, covered, for 5 minutes. Season with salt and pepper to taste. Combine the mayonnaise, mustard and $1/4$ teaspoon salt in a bowl and mix well. Spread over the cauliflower. Sprinkle with the cheese. Microwave on Medium for 1 to 2 minutes or until the cheese is melted. **Serves 4.**

According to the U.S. Department of Agriculture, fresh mushrooms account for about 80 percent of the mushroom market, whereas thirty years ago, it was only a third. Mushrooms should be stored in paper bags in the refrigerator. To clean before use, wipe with a damp cloth, paper towel, or soft-bristled brush. Rinse quickly in cold water, but do not allow mushrooms to soak in water.

Corn with Green Chiles

1/2 onion
1 garlic clove, minced
1/4 cup (1/2 stick) butter
5 cups corn kernels
4 ounces cream cheese

1 (4-ounce) can chopped
    green chiles
1/4 cup bourbon
1/4 cup half-and-half

Sauté the onion and garlic in the butter in a 2-quart saucepan until tender. Add the corn and cook for 2 minutes, stirring frequently. Add the cream cheese and green chiles and cook just until the cream cheese is melted, stirring constantly. Combine the bourbon and half-and-half in a bowl and mix well. Add to the corn mixture. Simmer over low heat for 15 minutes, stirring occasionally. **Serves 8.**

Elegant Mushroom Casserole

16 ounces large mushrooms, sliced
2 tablespoons butter
1 cup sour cream
2 tablespoons all-purpose flour
1/4 teaspoon garlic salt
1/4 teaspoon black pepper

1/8 teaspoon cayenne pepper
1 tablespoon chopped fresh chives
1/2 cup (2 ounces) shredded sharp
    Cheddar cheese
1/2 cup (2 ounces) shredded
    Monterey Jack cheese

Sauté the mushrooms in the butter in a skillet until tender. Combine the sour cream, flour, garlic salt, black pepper, cayenne pepper and chives in a bowl and mix well. Stir into the mushroom mixture. Pour into a 1-quart baking dish. Sprinkle with the Cheddar cheese and Monterey Jack cheese. Bake at 350 degrees for 15 minutes or until the cheeses are melted. **Serves 4 to 6.**

Scalloped Artichoke Potatoes

5 large potatoes, peeled and cut into $^1/_2$-inch pieces
$^1/_2$ teaspoon salt
2 (10-ounce) cans condensed cream of mushroom soup
6 ounces light cream cheese, softened
2 teaspoons butter, softened
2 (14-ounce) cans artichoke hearts, drained and chopped
$^1/_2$ cup (2 ounces) shredded Jarlsberg cheese
$^1/_2$ cup sliced green onions
$^1/_4$ cup skim milk
$^1/_4$ teaspoon garlic salt
$^1/_4$ teaspoon pepper
$^1/_2$ cup (2 ounces) shredded Jarlsberg cheese
Chopped green onions (optional)

Combine the potatoes and enough cold water to cover in a saucepan.
Add the salt and bring to a boil. Reduce the heat. Simmer, covered, for
10 minutes or just until the potatoes are tender; drain. Rinse with cold
water; drain again.

Combine the soup, cream cheese, butter and artichokes in a bowl and
mix well. Stir in $^1/_2$ cup Jarlsberg cheese, the sliced green onions, milk, garlic
salt and pepper. Add the potatoes and mix gently. Spoon into a 2-quart
baking dish sprayed with nonstick cooking spray.

Bake at 350 degrees for 30 minutes or until hot and bubbly. Sprinkle with
$^1/_2$ cup Jarlsberg cheese. Bake for 5 minutes or until the cheese is melted.
Sprinkle with a small amount of chopped green onions. **Serves 8.**

Lemon Horseradish New Potatoes

1/4 cup (1/2 stick) butter
2 tablespoons prepared horseradish
2 tablespoons fresh lemon juice
1/2 teaspoon salt
1/4 teaspoon pepper
11/2 pounds new potatoes, scrubbed

Melt the butter in a 2-quart baking dish. Stir in the horseradish, lemon juice, salt and pepper. Add the potatoes and toss to coat. Bake, covered, at 350 degrees for 1 hour or until the potatoes are tender. **Serves 4.**

Spanish Squash

6 zucchini, chopped
1 onion, chopped
1/4 cup (1/2 stick) margarine
Salt and pepper to taste
1 can whole kernel corn, drained
1 (4-ounce) can chopped green chiles
1 cup (4 ounces) shredded cheese

Sauté the zucchini and onion in the margarine in a saucepan until tender. Season with salt and pepper. Add the corn and green chiles and mix well. Spoon into a baking dish. Sprinkle with the cheese. Bake at 350 degrees until the cheese is melted. **Serves 10.**

Spinach Madeline

2 packages frozen chopped spinach, thawed
^{1}/4 cup (^{1}/2 stick) butter
2 tablespoons all-purpose flour
2 tablespoons chopped onion
^{1}/2 cup evaporated milk
1 teaspoon Worcestershire sauce
^{1}/2 teaspoon pepper
^{3}/4 teaspoon celery salt
1 (6-ounce) roll garlic cheese, chopped
6 ounces Velveeta cheese with jalapeño chiles, cubed
Bread crumbs
Grated Parmesan cheese

To stem spinach, fold the leaf in half at the stem and pull the stem down the length of the leaf. Small leaves do not have to be stemmed.

Squeeze the spinach to remove any excess moisture. Melt the butter in a saucepan over low heat. Add the flour and stir until blended and smooth; do not brown. Stir in the onion. Add the evaporated milk gradually, stirring constantly to prevent lumps. Add the Worcestershire sauce, pepper, celery salt, garlic cheese and Velveeta cheese and mix well. Cook until the cheeses are melted, stirring constantly. Add the spinach and mix well. Spoon into a buttered 9×9-inch baking dish. Sprinkle with bread crumbs and Parmesan cheese. Bake at 350 degrees for 15 minutes. You may freeze the mixture ahead of time, adjusting the baking time as needed. ***Serves 4 to 6.***

Squash Casserole

4 yellow squash, sliced
2 zucchini, sliced
1 large onion, chopped
1/2 cup (1 stick) butter
2 tablespoons sugar
1 tablespoon salt
1 cup (4 ounces) shredded sharp New York Cheddar cheese
1 cup (4 ounces) shredded Velveeta cheese
1 cup half-and-half

Combine the squash, zucchini and enough water to cover in a saucepan. Bring to a boil. Cook until tender; drain. Mash the squash mixture in a bowl. Sauté the onion in 1 tablespoon of the butter in a skillet until tender. Stir in the sugar and salt. Add to the squash mixture and mix well. Layer the squash mixture and cheeses 1/2 at a time in a buttered baking dish, dotting each layer with 1/2 of the remaining butter. Pour the half-and-half over the top. Bake at 350 degrees for 45 minutes. **Serves 8 to 10.**

Yellow Squash and Tomato Layers

5 yellow squash, sliced
5 tomatoes, sliced
Garlic salt to taste
2 cups (8 ounces) shredded Monterey Jack cheese
5 jalapeño chiles, sliced (optional)

Layer 1/2 of the squash and tomatoes in a 9×13-inch baking dish sprayed with nonstick cooking spray. Sprinkle with garlic salt, 1/2 of the cheese and 1/2 of the jalapeño chiles. Repeat the procedure with the remaining squash, tomatoes, garlic salt, cheese and jalapeño chiles. Bake at 350 degrees for 20 to 25 minutes. **Serves 6 to 8.**

Brown Sugar Sweet Potato Sticks

6 small sweet potatoes, scrubbed
1 tablespoon butter
1/4 cup chopped walnuts
1/4 cup plus 2 tablespoons packed light brown sugar
1/2 teaspoon salt
1/4 teaspoon pepper
1/4 teaspoon ground allspice
2 tablespoons cider vinegar

Pierce the sweet potatoes all over with a fork. Place on paper towels in a microwave. Microwave on High just until heated through, turning halfway through the cooking time; the sweet potatoes should still be firm. Let stand until cool. Cut each sweet potato lengthwise into quarters. Melt the butter in a skillet. Add the walnuts, brown sugar, salt, pepper, allspice and vinegar. Cook the glaze until the brown sugar is dissolved, stirring constantly. Remove from the heat. Heat coals to medium on a grill or preheat a gas grill to medium-high. Brush the cut sides of the sweet potatoes with the glaze, reserving the walnuts. Grill the sweet potatoes cut sides down for 5 minutes. Turn the sweet potatoes so the remaining cut sides are down and grill for 5 minutes. Turn skin sides down and brush with the remaining glaze. Grill until tender. Remove to a serving plate. Spoon the walnuts and remaining glaze over the sweet potatoes. Serve immediately. **Serves 8.**

Sweet Potato Casserole

SWEET POTATOES
3 cups mashed cooked
   sweet potatoes
1 cup sugar
2 eggs, beaten
1/2 cup (1 stick) margarine, melted
1 cup flaked coconut
1 teaspoon vanilla extract
1 teaspoon salt
1/4 cup milk or orange juice

TOPPING
1 cup chopped pecans
1/2 cup (1 stick) margarine, melted
1 cup packed brown sugar
1/2 cup all-purpose flour

FOR THE SWEET POTATOES, combine the sweet potatoes, sugar, eggs, margarine, coconut, vanilla, salt and milk in a bowl and mix well. Spoon into a buttered 9×13-inch baking dish.

FOR THE TOPPING, combine the pecans, margarine, brown sugar and flour in a bowl and mix well.

Spread the topping over the sweet potato mixture. Bake at 350 degrees for 20 to 25 minutes or until light brown. ***Serves 6 to 8.***

Tomato Pie

1 unbaked pie shell
4 or 5 medium tomatoes, peeled
   and cut into 1/2-inch slices
1 cup (4 ounces) shredded
   Cheddar cheese

1/2 cup mayonnaise
1 or 2 green onions, minced
2 tablespoons minced fresh parsley

Bake the pie shell using the package directions. Layer the tomatoes in the piecrust. Sprinkle with the cheese. Combine the mayonnaise, green onions and parsley in a bowl and mix well. Spread over the cheese. Bake in the lower half of the oven at 350 degrees for 30 minutes. Serve immediately. ***Serves 6 to 8.***

Asian Vegetable Medley

VEGETABLE MEDLEY

1 cup rice, cooked and cooled

1 can sliced water chestnuts, drained

1 (16-ounce) can whole kernel corn, drained

1 (16-ounce) can sliced carrots, drained

1 cup chopped celery

1/2 cup chopped green bell pepper

1/2 cup chopped onion

MARINADE

1 cup white vinegar

1/2 cup water

1/2 cup canola oil

1 cup sugar

2 teaspoons salt

1/2 teaspoon pepper

Melt a few pats of butter in a plastic freezer bag in the microwave when serving corn on the cob. Drop cooked ears in the bag and roll them around to distribute the butter evenly.

FOR THE VEGETABLE MEDLEY, combine the rice, water chestnuts, corn, carrots, celery, bell pepper and onion in a bowl and mix well.

FOR THE MARINADE, combine the vinegar, water, canola oil, sugar, salt and pepper in a saucepan and mix well. Bring to a boil; stir.

Pour the marinade over the rice mixture and mix well. Chill, covered, for several hours. You may store the mixture in the refrigerator, covered, for several days. You may substitute 1 cup cooked sliced fresh carrots for the canned carrots. **Serves 12 to 15.**

Macaroni and Cheese Casserole

8 ounces elbow macaroni
2 tablespoons onion
3 tablespoons butter
1/4 to 1/3 cup flour
2 cups milk
8 ounces (2 cups) shredded sharp Cheddar cheese
2 1/3 tablespoons butter
3/4 cup bread crumbs
1/4 teaspoon paprika

Cook the macaroni using the package directions; drain. Sauté the onion in 3 tablespoons butter in a saucepan until tender. Stir in enough of the flour to make of the desired consistency. Add the milk gradually, stirring constantly. Cook the white sauce until thickened, stirring constantly. Layer the macaroni, white sauce and cheese 1/3 at a time in a 2-quart baking dish. Melt 2 1/3 tablespoons butter in a saucepan. Remove from the heat. Stir in the bread crumbs. Spoon evenly over the top of the cheese. Sprinkle with the paprika. Bake at 375 degrees for 25 to 30 minutes or until bubbly and brown. ***Serves 8.***

Baked Rice Casserole

2 cans French onion soup
2 cans beef broth
2 cups rice
1 (4-ounce) can sliced mushrooms, drained (optional)
1 package slivered almonds
1/2 cup (1 stick) butter or margarine, sliced

Combine the French onion soup, beef broth, rice, mushrooms, almonds and butter in a bowl and mix well. Spoon into a baking dish. Bake, covered, at 325 degrees for 1 1/2 hours. ***Serves 8 to 10.***

Spanish Rice

2 slices bacon
1/4 cup chopped green bell pepper
1/4 cup chopped onion
1 can spicy vegetable juice cocktail
1 cup instant rice
1 teaspoon seasoned salt

Sauté the bacon in a skillet until crisp; drain, reserving the drippings in the skillet. Let the bacon stand until cool. Crumble the bacon. Sauté the bell pepper and onion in the reserved bacon drippings until tender. Bring the vegetable juice cocktail to a boil in a saucepan. Stir in the bell pepper mixture, rice and seasoned salt. Remove from the heat. Let stand, covered, for 5 to 10 minutes or until the rice is tender. Sprinkle with the bacon. You may substitute plain vegetable juice cocktail for the spicy vegetable juice cocktail. **Serves 4.**

Roasting peppers on a grill or under a broiler creates a hearty, smoky flavor. Place peppers directly on a hot grill. Grill for 10 to 15 minutes or broil for 15 to 20 minutes or until charred. Cover the charred peppers tightly with plastic wrap or place in a sealed plastic bag to produce steam that allows the skin to come off more easily.

Easy Rice Pilaf

1 cup rice
1 can beef consommé
1/4 cup (1/2 stick) butter, melted
1 envelope onion soup mix
1 (4-ounce) can sliced mushrooms, drained
1 mushroom can water

Combine the rice, beef consommé, butter, soup mix, mushrooms and water in a bowl and mix well. Spoon into a baking dish. Bake at 350 degrees for 1 hour. **Serves 6.**

Corn Bread Dressing

2 ribs celery, chopped
1/2 onion, chopped
1/2 cup sliced mushrooms
2 small zucchini, chopped
1 package corn bread mix
4 or 5 slices white bread, torn
2 1/2 cups chicken broth
2 eggs, beaten
3 eggs, hard-cooked and chopped
1 tablespoon sage
1 teaspoon poultry seasoning
1 teaspoon salt
1/2 teaspoon pepper

Sauté the celery, onion, mushrooms and zucchini in a nonstick skillet until tender. Prepare and bake the corn bread mix using the package directions. Let stand until cool. Crumble the corn bread into a bowl. Add the white bread and the celery mixture and mix well. Add the chicken broth, 2 beaten eggs, 3 hard-cooked eggs, the sage, poultry seasoning, salt and pepper and mix well. Spoon into an 11×14-inch baking dish. Bake at 375 degrees for 45 to 60 minutes or until done to taste. **Serves 12.**

Spoon Bread

2 cups milk
1 cup cornmeal
1 teaspoon baking powder
1 teaspoon salt
1 cup milk
3 egg yolks, beaten
2 tablespoons butter, melted
3 egg whites, stiffly beaten

Combine 2 cups milk and the cornmeal in a saucepan. Cook until thickened but not mushy, stirring constantly. Add the baking powder and salt and mix well. Stir in 1 cup milk. Add the egg yolks and butter and mix well. Fold in the egg whites. Pour into a greased 2-quart baking dish. Bake at 450 degrees for 10 minutes. Reduce the oven temperature to 350 degrees. Continue to bake for 50 minutes. **Serves 6.**

Country White Bread

2 envelopes yeast
1 tablespoon sugar
$^{1}/_{2}$ cup warm water
2 cups buttermilk, warmed
2 eggs
1$^{1}/_{2}$ teaspoons salt
$^{1}/_{4}$ cup honey
$^{1}/_{2}$ cup (1 stick) butter, melted
8 to 9 cups all-purpose flour
1 egg
1 tablespoon water
Melted butter for brushing

There are various ways of using an egg wash to get the proper color and effect of the dish. Beat an egg with a little water to produce a shine and some browning. For a darker shine, use milk instead of water. For less color, use only the white of the egg and not the yolk.

Dissolve the yeast and sugar in the warm water in a bowl. Let stand for 10 minutes. Combine the yeast mixture, buttermilk, 2 eggs, the salt, honey, $^{1}/_{2}$ cup butter and 4 cups of the flour in a bowl and mix well. Stir in enough of the remaining flour to form a stiff dough. Knead the dough on a lightly floured surface. Place in a greased bowl, turning to coat the surface. Let rise for about 1 hour.

Punch down the dough. Let rise for 30 minutes. Shape the dough into 36 rolls. Arrange in greased or buttered baking pans. Let rise for about 20 minutes. Combine 1 egg and the water in a bowl and mix well. Brush the egg wash gently over the rolls.

Bake at 350 degrees for 12 to 15 minutes. Remove to a wire rack and brush with melted butter. Let stand until completely cool. Place in sealable plastic bags and refrigerate or freeze until ready to rewarm. Arrange chilled or thawed rolls on a baking sheet and cover with foil. Bake at 300 degrees for about 10 to 15 minutes.

You may use the dough to make loaves of bread, Cinnamon Rolls (see page 189) or cheese rolls. To make loaves, shape the dough into 3 round loaves and place each loaf in an 8-inch round baking pan. Let rise for 45 minutes to 1 hour, and then bake at 375 degrees for 35 to 40 minutes. **Makes 3 dozen rolls.**

Monkey Bread

1 cake yeast
1/4 cup warm water
1/2 cup (1 stick) butter, melted
1 cup milk, scalded
2 eggs, beaten
3 tablespoons sugar
1 teaspoon salt
4 cups unsifted all-purpose flour
Melted butter or margarine

Dissolve the yeast in the warm water in a bowl. Combine the butter and milk in a mixing bowl. Beat in the yeast mixture, eggs, sugar and salt until well mixed. Add 2 cups of the flour gradually, beating constantly. Beat in 1 cup of the flour. Add the remaining flour and beat until smooth. Chill, covered, for 8 to 10 hours.

Roll the dough 1/3 inch thick on a lightly floured surface. Cut into 1 1/2- to 2-inch squares. Dip each square into melted butter and arrange 1 layer of squares in each of two 8-inch tube pans. Repeat the layering procedure 2 times, arranging the squares to cover the spaces in the previous layer. Let rise, covered with a kitchen towel, for 1 1/2 to 2 hours or until the tube pans are filled.

Bake at 400 degrees for 12 to 15 minutes. Invert onto a plate. You may broil the bottom of the bread to brown, if desired. You may store the dough, covered, in the refrigerator for several days, or you may bake the bread and store, covered, in the refrigerator until ready to reheat. Wrap the chilled bread in foil to reheat. Use pasteurized eggs if you store the unbaked dough.
Serves 16.

Momma's Rolls

2 envelopes yeast
$^1/_2$ cup sugar
2 cups water, at 100 degrees
$^1/_4$ cup ($^1/_2$ stick) butter or margarine
1 egg
2 teaspoons salt
$5^1/_2$ cups (or more) all-purpose flour

Dissolve the yeast and 1 tablespoon of the sugar in $^1/_2$ cup of the water in a bowl. Combine the remaining sugar, remaining water, butter, egg and salt in a mixing bowl and mix well. Stir in the yeast mixture. Add 3 cups of the flour and beat until smooth. Add the remaining flour and stir just until mixed, adding up to $^1/_2$ cup additional flour if the dough is too sticky. Place in a greased bowl, turning to coat the surface. Cover with plastic wrap. Let rise for 2 to 24 hours in the refrigerator. Punch down the dough. Shape into rolls and arrange in 4 baking pans. Bake at 400 degrees for 8 to 10 minutes. **Makes 32 rolls.**

Dinner Rolls

1/2 cup sugar
1 1/2 teaspoons salt
1 envelope yeast
2 cups lukewarm water
5 cups all-purpose flour
1 egg
1/2 cup shortening, melted and cooled

Combine the sugar and salt in a bowl and mix well. Dissolve the yeast
in the lukewarm water in a bowl. Add to the sugar mixture and mix well.
Stir in 3 cups of the flour. Add the egg and shortening and mix well. Add
the remaining flour and mix well. Chill, covered with plastic wrap, for
1 hour or longer. Shape into rolls. Arrange in a greased baking pan. Bake at
375 degrees for 20 minutes or until golden brown. You may sprinkle the
dough with grated Parmesan cheese, crushed rosemary or sesame seeds before
baking. ***Makes 3 dozen rolls.***

Creamed Corn Biscuits

1/4 cup (1/2 stick) butter
1 1/2 cups baking mix
1 (8-ounce) can cream-style corn
Dash of cayenne pepper (optional)

Melt the butter in a 10×15-inch baking pan. Combine the baking mix, corn and cayenne pepper in a bowl and mix well; the mixture will be thick and sticky. Drop by heaping teaspoonfuls into the melted butter, rolling to coat. Bake at 400 degrees for 15 to 20 minutes or until golden brown. Serve immediately. **Makes (about) 15 biscuits.**

Giant Popovers

6 eggs
2 cups milk
6 tablespoons butter, melted
2 cups all-purpose flour
1 teaspoon salt

Beat the eggs at low speed in a mixing bowl until frothy. Beat in the milk and butter. Beat in the flour and salt. Pour by 3/4 cupfuls into greased popover cups or custard cups. Place in a 10×15-inch baking pan. Bake at 375 degrees for 1 hour. Cut a small slit in the top of each popover to allow the steam to escape. Bake for 10 minutes longer. Serve hot with butter. **Makes 1 dozen popovers.**

Pull-Away Bread

1/4 cup grated Parmesan cheese
3 tablespoons sesame seeds
1 teaspoon basil
1 (25-ounce) package frozen roll dough
3 tablespoons butter, melted

Combine the cheese, sesame seeds and basil in a bowl and mix well.
Sprinkle 1/3 of the cheese mixture over the bottom of a 12-cup bundt pan.
Arrange 1/2 of the frozen rolls in the prepared pan. Drizzle with 1/2 of the
butter and sprinkle with 1/2 of the remaining cheese mixture. Repeat the
procedure using the remaining rolls, butter and cheese mixture. Let rise in
a warm place for 3 to 4 hours or until doubled in bulk. Bake at 350 degrees
for 20 minutes. Cover with foil to prevent overbrowning and bake for
10 minutes longer. Run a knife around the edge of the bread to loosen
and invert onto a serving plate. **Serves 8.**

Rise and Shine

Breakfast and Brunch

Brunch for a Bunch

Photograph courtesy of Christopher Bentley

To decorate a table for a spring gathering, begin with white as a basic color, because it can be dressed up or down. Then add an accent color, depending on your theme. If you have a favorite tray or item, use that as your focal color. Votives can be added as an inexpensive accent.

Breakfast Berry Smoothie

3 cups frozen berries (strawberries or mixed berries)
1 ripe banana, peeled and frozen
$1/2$ cup milk
$1/2$ cup apple juice or cranberry juice
1 tablespoon sugar
1 tablespoon lemon juice
$1/2$ cup ice cubes or crushed ice

Combine the berries, banana, milk, apple juice, sugar, lemon juice and ice in a blender and process until smooth. Serve immediately. *Serves 1.*

Hard cider is usually made from fermented apple juice. The alcohol content can vary, but is usually comparable to that of beer.

Peach Hot Tea Mix

4 (4-ounce) packages peach gelatin
$13/4$ cups sugar
$1/2$ cup instant tea granules
$1/2$ cup lemonade mix

Combine the gelatin, sugar, tea granules and lemonade mix in a bowl and mix well. Store in an airtight container. To serve, combine 1 tablespoon of the gelatin mixture with 6 ounces hot water in a teacup and stir until dissolved. *Serves 70 to 80.*

Ham and Cheese Puffs

2 sheets frozen puff pastry, thawed
15 (1-ounce) slices cooked ham
8 (3/4-ounce) slices Swiss cheese
1/3 cup peach preserves
1/3 cup spicy mustard
2 egg yolks, beaten

Roll 1 of the puff pastry sheets into a 9×18-inch rectangle on a lightly floured surface. Cut fifteen 3-inch squares from the dough, reserving the remaining dough. Cut fifteen 3/4-inch circles from the reserved dough. Repeat the procedure using the remaining puff pastry sheet. Cut each ham slice and each cheese slice into 4 squares. Combine the peach preserves and spicy mustard in a bowl and mix well. Spread about 1/2 teaspoon of the mixture over each square of dough, leaving a 3/4-inch border. Layer 1 ham square and 1 cheese square on 1 dough square. Add 1 ham square on the diagonal. Brush the border of the dough with egg yolks. Bring the 4 corners together and seal the seams. Brush 1 side of 1 dough circle with egg yolks. Place egg side down on top of the puff, pressing lightly in the center. Repeat the procedure using the remaining ingredients, reserving the 2 leftover cheese squares for another purpose. Arrange on a baking sheet. Freeze for 15 minutes or longer. Bake at 425 degrees for 15 to 17 minutes. **Makes 30 puffs.**

Texas is the second largest agricultural state in the United States, accounting for about 7 percent of the total U.S. agricultural income.

—Texas Department of Agriculture

Sausage Swirls

3³/4 cups all-purpose flour
1/4 cup cornmeal
1/4 cup sugar
2 tablespoons baking powder
1 teaspoon salt

2/3 cup vegetable oil
2/3 to 1 cup milk
2 pounds bulk pork sausage
(preferably Owens)

Sift the flour, cornmeal, sugar, baking powder and salt into a bowl. Stir in the oil and enough of the milk to make a stiff dough. Divide the dough into 2 portions. Roll 1 of the dough portions into a 10×18-inch rectangle on a work surface. Spread 1/2 of the sausage over the rectangle. Roll as for a jelly roll, starting at 1 long side. Repeat the procedure with the remaining dough and remaining sausage. Chill or freeze, wrapped in waxed paper, just until firm. Cut into 1/4-inch slices and arrange on baking sheets. Bake at 375 degrees for 15 to 20 minutes or until light brown. **Makes 72 swirls.**

Surprisingly Sensational Chutney Cheese Spread

16 ounces cream cheese, softened
1/2 cup Old Farmhouse chutney
1/4 cup finely sliced green onions
including light green tops
1 garlic clove, minced
1/2 cup (2 ounces) shredded
Cheddar cheese

1/2 cup (2 ounces) shredded
Monterey Jack cheese
Salt and pepper to taste
1 cup chopped pecans

Beat the cream cheese in a mixing bowl until fluffy. Add the chutney, green onions, garlic, Cheddar cheese, Monterey Jack cheese, salt and pepper and mix well. Add the pecans and mix well. Spoon into a serving dish. Serve with crackers or Granny Smith apples. You may shape the cream cheese mixture into a ball, reserving the pecans for coating the cheese ball; chill the mixture, covered, for 30 minutes or until firm before shaping into a ball. If you use a different brand of chutney, reduce the amount to 1/4 cup. **Serves 20.**

Chicken and Chiles Cheese Ball

8 ounces cream cheese, softened
1/2 cup finely chopped cooked chicken, or
    1 (5-ounce) can chicken, drained and flaked
2 to 3 tablespoons chopped green chiles, drained
1 tablespoon finely chopped onion
1 teaspoon chicken bouillon granules
1/4 teaspoon garlic powder
1/2 cup finely chopped nuts

Combine the cream cheese, chicken, green chiles, onion, bouillon granules and garlic powder in a bowl and mix well. Shape into a ball and coat with the nuts. Chill, covered, until serving time. Serve with crackers. Refrigerate any leftovers. *Serves 8 to 10.*

Chocolate Chip Cheese Ball

8 ounces cream cheese, softened
1/2 cup (1 stick) butter, softened
3/4 cup confectioners' sugar
3 tablespoons brown sugar
1 teaspoon vanilla extract
3/4 cup miniature chocolate chips
3/4 cup chopped pecans

Combine the cream cheese and butter in a mixing bowl and beat until smooth. Beat in the confectioners' sugar, brown sugar and vanilla. Stir in the chocolate chips. Chill, wrapped in plastic wrap, for 2 hours. Shape into a ball and coat with the pecans. Serve with graham crackers. You may stir the pecans into the cream cheese mixture and serve as a dip. *Serves 6 to 8.*

Green Chile and Cheese Strata

6 flour tortillas
8 green chiles, roasted, peeled and chopped, or
    2 (8-ounce) cans chopped green chiles
3 cups (12 ounces) shredded
    Monterey Jack cheese
6 eggs, beaten
6 egg whites, beaten
1 1/2 cups milk
1/2 teaspoon salt
1/2 teaspoon white pepper

Arrange 3 of the tortillas on the bottom of a greased 9×13-inch baking
dish, cutting to fit without overlapping. Sprinkle with 1/2 of the green chiles
and 1/2 of the cheese. Repeat the layers of tortillas, green chiles and cheese.
Combine the eggs, egg whites, milk, salt and white pepper in a bowl and mix
well. Pour over the layers. Chill, covered, for 30 minutes to 10 hours. Bake
at 350 degrees for 30 minutes or until slightly puffed and bubbly. Let stand to
cool for 5 minutes before serving. **Serves 8 to 10.**

Spinach Bacon Quiche

2 unbaked (9-inch) pie shells
1 (12-ounce) package frozen chopped spinach,
   thawed
1 tablespoon margarine
1/3 cup chopped onion
3/4 cup half-and-half
2 eggs
1 teaspoon garlic salt
1/8 teaspoon pepper
1/4 teaspoon basil
1 cup ricotta cheese
6 slices bacon, crisp-cooked and crumbled

Bacon can actually be cooked in a preheated 350-degree oven, thus avoiding messy splatters or griddle cleanup. Place bacon on a foil-lined jelly roll pan or other pan with deep sides. Cook for 20 minutes or to desired crispness. Remove to a plate lined with paper towels to absorb grease; then simply throw away the foil.

Bake the pie shells at 425 degrees for 10 minutes. Maintain the oven temperature. Drain the spinach, pressing to remove any excess moisture. Melt the margarine in a skillet. Cook the onion in the hot margarine for 3 minutes, stirring frequently. Add the half-and-half and cook over medium heat until bubbly around the edge. Combine the eggs, garlic salt, pepper and basil in a blender and process until blended. Add the ricotta cheese and process until blended. Add the onion mixture and mix well. Stir in the spinach and bacon. Pour equal portions of the mixture into each pie shell. Bake for 35 minutes or just until set. Let stand to cool slightly before serving. **Serves 12.**

Crustless Veggie Quiche

1 (10-ounce) package frozen
    chopped spinach, thawed
1 cup frozen chopped broccoli,
    thawed
3 ounces light cream cheese,
    softened
1 cup milk
4 eggs
1/4 teaspoon pepper
3 cups (12 ounces) shredded Cheddar cheese
1 small onion, finely chopped
1 (7-ounce) can mushrooms, drained and sliced

Drain the spinach and broccoli, squeezing the spinach to remove any excess moisture. Beat the cream cheese in a mixing bowl. Add the milk, eggs and pepper and beat until smooth. Stir in the spinach, broccoli, Cheddar cheese, onion and mushrooms. Pour into a 10-inch quiche pan sprayed with nonstick cooking spray. Bake at 350 degrees for 45 to 50 minutes or until a knife inserted in the center comes out clean. **Serves 8.**

Breakfast Pizza

2 pounds bulk pork sausage
2 (6-ounce) packages pizza crust mix
1 cup hot water
2 cups frozen shredded hash brown potatoes
5 eggs
1 cup pasteurized egg substitute
1/2 cup milk
1/4 teaspoon salt
1/4 teaspoon pepper
2 cups (8 ounces) shredded Cheddar cheese
1/2 cup (2 ounces) grated Parmesan cheese

Brown the sausage in a skillet, stirring until crumbly; drain. Prepare the pizza crust mix with the hot water using the package directions. Spread the dough over the bottom and up the sides of a 10×15-inch baking pan. Spread the sausage evenly over the dough. Sprinkle with the potatoes. Combine the eggs, egg substitute, milk, salt and pepper in a bowl and mix well. Pour evenly over the potatoes. Sprinkle with the Cheddar cheese and Parmesan cheese. Bake at 425 degrees for 45 minutes or until the eggs are set. You may substitute 5 eggs for the egg substitute; adjust the baking time accordingly. **Serves 24.**

Herbed Brunch Casserole

2 pounds bulk pork sausage

2¹/2 cups herb-seasoned croutons

2 cups (8 ounces) shredded sharp
  Cheddar cheese

4 ounces sliced mushrooms

6 eggs

2¹/2 cups milk

1 (10-ounce) can condensed cream of
  mushroom soup

2³/4 teaspoons dry mustard

Brown the sausage in a skillet, stirring until crumbly; drain. Arrange the croutons in a single layer in a greased 9×13-inch baking dish. Sprinkle evenly with the cheese, mushrooms and sausage. Combine the eggs, milk, soup and dry mustard in a bowl and mix well. Pour evenly over the sausage. Bake at 300 degrees for 1¹/2 hours or until set. You may chill the casserole, covered, for 8 to 10 hours before baking. *Serves 12 to 15.*

Cinnamon Raisin and Pecan Casserole

CASSEROLE

2 packages Little Sizzlers sausage, cubed

1 loaf cinnamon raisin bread, cubed

6 eggs

$1^1/2$ cups milk

$1^1/2$ cups half-and-half

1 teaspoon vanilla extract

$1/4$ teaspoon nutmeg

$1/4$ teaspoon ground cinnamon

TOPPING

1 cup packed brown sugar

1 cup coarsely chopped pecans

$1/2$ cup (1 stick) butter, softened

2 tablespoons maple syrup

FOR THE CASSEROLE, brown the sausage in a skillet; drain. Layer the bread and sausage in a greased 9×13-inch baking pan. Combine the eggs, milk, half-and-half, vanilla, nutmeg and cinnamon in a bowl and mix well. Pour evenly over the sausage. Chill, covered, for 8 to 10 hours.

FOR THE TOPPING, combine the brown sugar, pecans, butter and maple syrup in a bowl and mix well.

Sprinkle the topping over the top of the casserole. Bake at 350 degrees for 35 to 40 minutes. *Serves 8 to 10.*

Sinful Potatoes

1 (32-ounce) package frozen shredded
   hash brown potatoes
1 (10-ounce) can condensed cream of
   celery soup
1 cup sour cream
2 cups (8 ounces) shredded Colby Jack cheese
^{1}/4 cup (^{1}/2 stick) butter, melted
1 onion, chopped
1 (4-ounce) can chopped green chiles
1^1/2 teaspoons salt
2 cups crushed cornflakes
^{1}/2 cup (1 stick) butter, melted

Combine the potatoes, soup, sour cream, cheese, ^{1}/4 cup butter, the onion,
green chiles and salt in a bowl and mix well. Grease a 9×13-inch baking pan
or spray with nonstick cooking spray. Spoon the potato mixture into the pan.
Combine the cornflakes and ^{1}/2 cup butter in a bowl and mix well. Sprinkle
evenly over the potato mixture. Bake at 350 degrees for 45 minutes or until
bubbly. **Serves 10.**

*To avoid irritation of the
eyes when chopping onions,
light a candle nearby before
chopping. The flame from
the candle helps to neutralize
the sulfuric fumes from
the onion.*

Sour Cream Coffee Cake

TOPPING
1/2 cup chopped pecans
2 teaspoons cinnamon
1/4 cup packed brown sugar

COFFEE CAKE
1 cup (2 sticks) butter, softened
2 cups sugar
2 eggs
1 cup sour cream
1 teaspoon vanilla extract
2 cups all-purpose flour
1 teaspoon baking powder
Confectioners' sugar (optional)

FOR THE TOPPING, combine the pecans, cinnamon and brown sugar in a bowl and mix well.

FOR THE COFFEE CAKE, cream the butter and sugar in a mixing bowl. Beat in the eggs 1 at a time. Fold in the sour cream and vanilla. Sift the flour and baking powder together. Stir into the butter mixture. Pour 1/2 of the batter into a greased and floured bundt or 10-inch tube pan.

Sprinkle 1/2 of the topping over the coffee cake batter. Pour the remaining batter over the topping and sprinkle with the remaining topping. Bake at 350 degrees for 55 to 60 minutes. Let stand until cool. Sprinkle with confectioners' sugar. **Serves 12 to 16.**

Cinnamon Rolls

$1/3$ recipe Country White Bread dough
   (page 168)
1 cup raisins, scalded and patted dry
Melted butter for brushing
$1/2$ cup granulated sugar
1 tablespoon ground cinnamon
$1/2$ cup nuts (optional)
2 tablespoons butter, melted
1 cup confectioners' sugar
$1/2$ teaspoon vanilla extract
2 tablespoons milk

Place the Country White Bread dough on a work surface. Sprinkle the top
of the dough with the raisins and knead until well mixed. Let stand, covered,
for a few minutes. Roll the dough into a 9×15-inch rectangle. Brush with
melted butter, leaving a $1/2$-inch border. Combine the sugar and cinnamon
and mix well. Sprinkle over the dough. Sprinkle with the nuts. Roll from
1 long side as for a jelly roll, sealing the seam. Cut into 1-inch slices and
arrange in 2 greased round or square pans. Let rise, covered, for about
30 minutes. Bake at 350 degrees for 25 minutes; do not overbake. Remove
to a serving plate. Combine 2 tablespoons butter, the confectioners' sugar,
vanilla and milk in a bowl and mix well. Spread over the warm rolls.
You may brush the rolls with additional butter before spreading with the
glaze. These rolls may be frozen; brush with melted butter before reheating.
Makes 15 rolls.

Rich Swedish Cream Dough

1 envelope yeast
$^1/_4$ cup water, at 110 degrees
1 cup heavy cream
$^1/_4$ cup evaporated milk
3 egg yolks
$3^1/_3$ cups all-purpose flour
$^1/_4$ cup sugar
1 teaspoon salt
$^1/_2$ cup (1 stick) butter
Butter for spreading

Dissolve the yeast in the water in a bowl. Combine the yeast mixture, cream, evaporated milk and egg yolks in a bowl and mix well. Combine the flour, sugar and salt in a bowl and mix well. Cut in $^1/_2$ cup butter using a pastry blender or 2 knives until the mixture resembles coarse crumbs. Add the yeast mixture and stir just until moistened. Spread with a small amount of butter to prevent drying. Chill, covered with plastic wrap, for 8 to 10 hours or for up to 4 days. Shape and bake as desired (see Bear Claws and Butterhorns on page 191). ***Makes variable servings.***

Bear Claws

1 cup almond paste or finely chopped pecans
1 cup confectioners' sugar
2 egg whites, lightly beaten
1/2 recipe Rich Swedish Cream Dough (page 190)
Granulated sugar
Sliced almonds

Combine the almond paste, confectioners' sugar and 1 of the egg whites in a mixing bowl and beat until smooth. Roll the Rich Swedish Cream Dough into a 12×24-inch rectangle on a floured surface. Cut into three 4×24-inch strips. Crumble equal portions of the almond paste mixture lengthwise down the center of each strip. Fold both long ends of each strip to the center to enclose the filling, sealing the seams. Cut each strip into 6 equal portions. Sprinkle with granulated sugar. Arrange on a greased baking sheet and curve each portion to form a fan. Brush with the remaining egg white. Let rise for 50 minutes. Bake at 350 degrees for 15 to 20 minutes. Sprinkle with almonds. You may omit the granulated sugar and drizzle the rolls with a confectioners' sugar icing after baking. **Makes 18 rolls.**

To make **Butterhorns**, roll 1/4 recipe Rich Swedish Cream Dough into an 8-inch circle and brush with melted butter. Cut into 8 wedges and roll up each wedge, starting at the wide end and ending at the point. Place point side down on a lightly greased baking sheet, curving to form a crescent. Let rise for 50 minutes. Bake at 350 degrees for 15 to 20 minutes. **Makes 8 rolls.**

Maple Nut Coffee Twist

*You may make an **Apricot Twist** by substituting cooked sweetened apricots for the filling and omitting the maple flavoring.*

FILLING
1/2 cup sugar
1 teaspoon maple flavoring
1 teaspoon ground cinnamon
1/3 cup chopped nuts

COFFEE CAKE
1 package hot roll mix
3/4 cup warm water
1 egg
3 tablespoons sugar
1 teaspoon maple flavoring
6 tablespoons butter, melted

GLAZE
1 1/2 cups confectioners' sugar
1/4 teaspoon maple flavoring
2 to 3 tablespoons milk

FOR THE FILLING, combine the sugar, maple flavoring, cinnamon and nuts in a bowl and mix well.

FOR THE COFFEE CAKE, dissolve the yeast from the hot roll mix in the warm water in a bowl. Stir in the egg, sugar and maple flavoring. Add the hot roll mix and mix well. Knead on a floured surface for 2 to 3 minutes. Place in a greased bowl. Let rise, covered, for 30 to 45 minutes. Divide into 3 equal portions and shape each portion into a ball. Roll 1 ball into a 12-inch circle on a lightly floured surface. Fit onto a greased pizza pan. Brush with 2 tablespoons of the butter and sprinkle with 1/3 cup of the filling. Repeat the procedure 2 times, using the remaining dough, butter and filling. Place a 2-inch glass open side down in the center of the layers and press lightly to score. Cut the layers into 16 wedges, starting from the outside edge and ending at the circle. Twist each wedge 5 times. Let rise for 30 to 45 minutes. Bake at 375 degrees for 20 to 25 minutes.

FOR THE GLAZE, combine the confectioners' sugar, maple flavoring and milk in a bowl and mix well. Drizzle the glaze over the warm coffee cake.
Serves 16.

Jamaican Jungle Bread

BREAD

1¹/2 cups all-purpose flour

1 cup rolled oats

¹/2 cup sugar

1 teaspoon baking soda

1 teaspoon baking powder

1¹/2 teaspoons ground cinnamon

¹/2 teaspoon salt

¹/2 cup flaked coconut

¹/2 cup chopped nuts

1 cup mashed bananas

1 (8-ounce) can crushed pineapple, drained

¹/4 cup vegetable oil

2 eggs

GLAZE

¹/2 cup confectioners' sugar

1 tablespoon margarine, softened

¹/2 teaspoon vanilla extract

1 to 2 teaspoons milk

FOR THE BREAD, combine the flour, oats, sugar, baking soda, baking powder, cinnamon, salt, coconut and nuts in a bowl and mix well. Combine the bananas, pineapple, oil and eggs in a bowl and mix well. Add to the flour mixture and stir just until mixed. Pour into a greased 5×9-inch loaf pan. Bake at 350 degrees for 1 hour. Cool in the pan for 5 minutes.

FOR THE GLAZE, combine the confectioners' sugar, margarine, vanilla and milk in a bowl and mix well.

Drizzle the glaze over the warm bread. *Serves 12.*

Banana Tea Bread

$^1/_2$ cup (1 stick) butter, softened
$1^1/_3$ cups sugar
2 eggs
$^1/_4$ cup sour cream
2 tablespoons milk
1 teaspoon almond extract
2 cups all-purpose flour
$1^1/_2$ teaspoons baking powder
$^1/_2$ teaspoon baking soda
$^1/_4$ teaspoon salt
1 cup mashed bananas
1 cup chopped pecans
Confectioners' sugar (optional)

Combine the butter and sugar in a mixing bowl and beat until smooth. Beat in the eggs, sour cream, milk, almond extract, flour, baking powder, baking soda and salt. Stir in the bananas and pecans. Pour into a greased and floured 5×9-inch loaf pan. Bake at 350 degrees until the bread tests done. Remove to a wire rack. Sprinkle with confectioners' sugar. **Serves 12.**

Hearty Banana Muffins

1/2 cup sugar
1 teaspoon baking soda
1/4 teaspoon salt
3/4 cup all-purpose flour
3/4 cup whole wheat flour
1/3 cup vegetable oil
1/4 cup milk
2 large bananas, mashed
1 teaspoon vanilla extract
1/3 cup raisins (optional)
Sugar for sprinkling (optional)

According to the Texas Department of Agriculture, Texas farmers grow more than sixty different commercial fruit and vegetable crops.

Combine 1/2 cup sugar, the baking soda, salt, all-purpose flour and whole wheat flour in a bowl and mix well. Add the oil, milk, bananas and vanilla and stir just until moistened. Fold in the raisins. Spray muffin cups with nonstick cooking spray and fill 2/3 full with batter. Sprinkle with a small amount of sugar. Bake at 375 degrees for 15 to 20 minutes or until golden brown. ***Makes 10 to 12 muffins.***

Icebox Bran Muffins

2 cups boiling water
2 1/2 cups All-Bran cereal
1 cup shortening
3 cups sugar
4 eggs

6 cups all-purpose flour
1 teaspoon salt
5 teaspoons baking soda
4 cups buttermilk

Pour the boiling water over the cereal in a bowl. Combine the shortening, sugar and eggs in a mixing bowl and beat until creamy. Combine the flour, salt and baking soda and mix well. Add the flour mixture to the shortening mixture alternately with the buttermilk. Stir in the cereal mixture. Fill muffin cups or custard cups 2/3 full with batter. Bake at 350 degrees for 20 minutes. You may add frozen blueberries or raspberries, or dried raisins or apricots, or fresh or frozen cranberries to the batter. You may cut the recipe in half. *Makes 3 dozen muffins.*

Pumpkin Bread

2 cups sugar
5 eggs
1 cup vegetable oil
2 cups canned pumpkin
2 cups all-purpose flour
1 teaspoon salt

1 teaspoon baking soda
1 1/2 teaspoons ground cinnamon
1 teaspoon nutmeg
2 (3-ounce) packages coconut
   instant pudding mix
1 cup chopped pecans

Combine the sugar, eggs, oil and pumpkin in a bowl and mix well. Combine the flour, salt, baking soda, cinnamon and nutmeg and mix well. Add the flour mixture to the sugar mixture and mix well. Stir in the pudding mix and pecans. Pour into two 5×9-inch loaf pans. Bake at 325 degrees for 50 to 60 minutes. *Serves 24.*

Cream Cheese Orange Breakfast Bread

3/4 cup granulated sugar

1/2 cup chopped pecans

1 tablespoon grated orange zest

2 (10-count) cans buttermilk biscuits

3 ounces block-style cream cheese, cut into 20 cubes

1/2 cup (1 stick) butter or margarine, melted

1 cup confectioners' sugar

2 tablespoons orange juice

Combine the granulated sugar, pecans and orange zest and mix well. Separate each biscuit into 2 layers. Place 1 cream cheese cube between the 2 layers and seal the seams. Dip in the butter and coat with the sugar mixture. Place on edge in a greased bundt pan. Drizzle with the remaining butter and sprinkle with the remaining sugar mixture. Bake at 350 degrees for 45 minutes or until golden brown. Combine the confectioners' sugar and orange juice in a bowl and mix well. Drizzle over the warm bread and serve. **Serves 10 to 12.**

Texas ranks first in the nation in the number of cattle and calves, accounting for 15 percent of the U.S. total. The Lone Star State is also the top producer of cotton, sheep, wool, goats, mohair, and horses. The state's top crops also include vegetables, citrus, corn, wheat, peanuts, pecans, grain sorghum, hay, and rice.

—*Texas Department of Agriculture*

Almond paste is a mixture of blanched ground almonds, glycerin, and sugar. It is similar to marzipan but is not as sweet.

Apricot Morning Treat

8 ounces cream cheese, softened
1 cup (2 sticks) margarine, softened
2 cups all-purpose flour
16 ounces apricot preserves
Brown sugar to taste
Chopped pecans to taste
1 cup confectioners' sugar
2 tablespoons milk

Cut the cream cheese and margarine into the flour in a bowl until crumbly. Divide into 3 equal portions. Roll each portion into a rectangle, 1/4 inch thick. Spread with equal portions of the apricot preserves. Sprinkle each with brown sugar and pecans. Roll each as for a jelly roll and place on a baking sheet coated with nonstick cooking spray. Bake at 325 degrees for 30 to 50 minutes or until golden brown. Let stand until cool. Combine the confectioners' sugar and milk in a bowl and mix well. Spread over the rolls. Cut into slices to serve. **Serves 24 to 36.**

Cinnamon Almond Shortbread

$1/2$ cup (1 stick) unsalted butter, softened
$1/4$ cup sugar
$1/2$ teaspoon vanilla extract
$1/8$ teaspoon salt
1 cup all-purpose flour
Sliced almonds
1 tablespoon cinnamon-sugar

Combine the butter, sugar, vanilla and salt in a bowl and mix using a fork. Add the flour and mix using a fork, then using hands. Place on an ungreased baking sheet and pat into a $1/4$-inch-thick 6-inch circle. Prick all over with a fork and crimp the edge. Score the dough into 8 portions. Sprinkle with the almonds and cinnamon-sugar. Bake at 375 degrees for 15 minutes or until the edge is golden brown. Let stand to cool for 10 minutes. Cut the warm shortbread along the score lines and serve. **Serves 8.**

Glenna's Sister's Coconut Cake

1 (2-layer) package white cake mix
3 packages frozen flaked coconut
3 cups sour cream
3 cups sugar

Prepare and bake the cake using the cake mix package directions for a 2-layer cake. Cut each layer horizontally into halves. Combine the coconut, sour cream and sugar in a bowl and mix well. Spread between the layers and over the top and side of the cake. Chill, covered, for 3 days before serving. **Serves 12.**

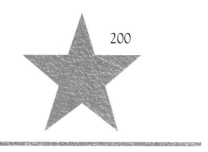

Watergate Dessert

1 cup all-purpose flour
$^1/_2$ cup (1 stick) margarine, softened
$^1/_4$ cup finely chopped pecans
8 ounces cream cheese, softened
1 cup confectioners' sugar
8 ounces whipped topping
2 (3-ounce) packages pistachio instant pudding mix
$2^1/_2$ cups milk
$^1/_4$ cup finely chopped pecans

Combine the flour, margarine and $^1/_4$ cup pecans in a bowl and mix well. Press over the bottom of a 9×13-inch baking pan. Bake at 350 degrees for 15 minutes. Let stand until completely cool. Combine the cream cheese, confectioners' sugar and $^1/_2$ of the whipped topping in a mixing bowl and beat until mixed. Spread over the cooled crust. Combine the pudding mix and milk in a mixing bowl and beat until mixed. Spread over the cream cheese mixture. Spread with the remaining whipped topping and sprinkle with $^1/_4$ cup pecans. Chill until serving time. You may substitute lemon or chocolate pudding mix for the pistachio pudding mix. **Serves 12 to 15.**

Pumpkin Soufflé

1 can pumpkin
3 eggs
1 can evaporated milk
1 (2-layer) package yellow cake mix
1 cup (2 sticks) butter, melted
1 teaspoon vanilla extract
$^{1}/_{2}$ cup chopped pecans (optional)

Combine the pumpkin, eggs and evaporated milk in a bowl and mix well. Pour into a greased 9×13-inch baking pan. Sprinkle with the cake mix. Combine the butter, vanilla and pecans in a bowl and mix well. Sprinkle over the top of the cake mix. Bake at 350 degrees for 1 hour. **Serves 12 to 15.**

A Perfect Ending

Desserts

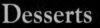

A Night in Italy

Photograph courtesy of Christopher Bentley

Any room can take on a glamorous or romantic feel with dimmed lights, well-placed candles, and large vases of flowers.

Tiramisu

8 ounces cream cheese, softened
2/3 cup sifted confectioners' sugar
1 cup whipped topping
3 egg whites
1/2 cup granulated sugar
1/4 cup water
1 tablespoon instant espresso granules
1 tablespoon granulated sugar
1/2 cup hot water
2 tablespoons Kahlúa
20 ladyfingers
1/2 cup whipped topping
1/2 teaspoon baking cocoa

The translation of tiramisu is "carry me up." This dessert is made by drizzling ladyfingers or a light sponge cake with a coffee mixture, and then layering the ladyfingers with a cream cheese mixture and sprinkling with baking cocoa. Tiramisu is similar to a trifle but is much lighter.

Combine the cream cheese and confectioners' sugar in a mixing bowl and beat at high speed until blended. Fold in 1 cup whipped topping. Combine the egg whites, 1/2 cup granulated sugar and 1/4 cup water in a double boiler over simmering water. Beat at high speed until stiff peaks form. Fold 1/4 of the egg white mixture into the cream cheese mixture. Fold in the remaining egg white mixture. Combine the espresso granules, 1 tablespoon granulated sugar, 1/2 cup hot water and the Kahlúa in a bowl and mix well. Cut the ladyfingers lengthwise into halves. Arrange 20 ladyfinger halves cut side up in an 8×8-inch pan. Drizzle with 1/2 of the espresso mixture. Spread with 1/2 of the cream cheese mixture. Repeat the procedure with the remaining ladyfinger halves, espresso mixture and cream cheese mixture. Spread with 1/2 cup whipped topping and sprinkle with the baking cocoa. Chill, covered with plastic wrap, for 2 hours. You may use low-fat cream cheese and whipped topping. **Serves 8.**

A bain-marie is a water bath
used for cooking delicate
dishes, usually containing
eggs. It keeps the dish from
scorching or curdling because
it cooks the dish in hot water,
providing a steam bath.

Guadalajara Flan

1 cup sugar
1 (14-ounce) can sweetened condensed milk
14 ounces milk
4 eggs
3 ounces cream cheese, softened
1 teaspoon Mexican vanilla or regular vanilla extract

Cook the sugar in a heavy cast-iron skillet just until dissolved, stirring
constantly; do not burn. Pour the caramelized sugar into a 9×13-inch baking
dish. Combine the sweetened condensed milk, milk, eggs, cream cheese and
vanilla in a blender and process until smooth. Pour over the caramelized
sugar. Cover with foil and place in a large pan of warm water. Bake at
325 degrees for 1 hour or until a knife inserted near the center comes
out clean. Chill, covered, until serving time. Invert onto a serving platter
and serve with whipped cream or fresh strawberries. **Serves 24.**

Chocolate Éclair Dessert

1 (6-ounce) package vanilla instant pudding mix
1 cup confectioners' sugar
3 cups milk
8 ounces whipped topping
1 package graham crackers
1 (16-ounce) can chocolate frosting

Combine the pudding mix, confectioners' sugar and milk in a mixing bowl
and beat until smooth. Fold in the whipped topping. Arrange a single layer
of graham crackers in a greased 9×13-inch dish. Spread with 1/2 of the
pudding mixture. Layer with graham crackers and the remaining pudding
mixture. Top with graham crackers. Chill, covered, until set. Spread with
the chocolate frosting. Chill, covered, until serving time. **Serves 24.**

Layered Raspberry Delight

1 cup (2 sticks) butter, melted
1¹/₂ cups all-purpose flour
2 tablespoons sugar
6 ounces cream cheese, softened
¹/₂ cup (1 stick) butter, melted
2 cups confectioners' sugar
¹/₂ teaspoon vanilla extract
1 cup chopped pecans or walnuts
1 (3-ounce) package raspberry gelatin
1 cup boiling water
2 (10-ounce) packages frozen raspberries in heavy syrup, thawed
2 cups whipping cream, sweetened and whipped

Combine 1 cup butter, the flour and sugar in a bowl and mix well. Spread over the bottom of a greased 9×13-inch baking pan. Bake at 350 degrees for 30 minutes or until light brown. Let stand until completely cool. Combine the cream cheese, ¹/₂ cup butter, the confectioners' sugar and vanilla in a mixing bowl and beat until smooth. Spread over the cooled crust and sprinkle with the pecans. Chill, covered, until set. Dissolve the gelatin in the boiling water in a bowl. Stir in the raspberries. Chill, covered, just until thickened. Spoon evenly over the cream cheese mixture. Chill, covered, until set. Cut into squares to serve. Top servings with sweetened whipped cream. You may substitute strawberries for the raspberries. **Serves 12.**

Coffee Toffee Crunch Ice Cream

2 cups light cream
1 (14-ounce) can sweetened condensed milk
2 tablespoons instant coffee granules
1 teaspoon vanilla extract
Pinch of salt
4 (1-ounce) Heath candy bars, coarsely chopped
1 tablespoon instant coffee granules

Combine the cream, sweetened condensed milk and 2 tablespoons coffee granules in a bowl and mix well. Stir in the vanilla and salt. Pour into an ice cream freezer. Freeze using the manufacturer's directions, adding the candy and 1 tablespoon coffee granules during the final few minutes of freezing time. *Makes 1 quart.*

Summer Mint Sherbet

2 cups water
2 cups sugar
1/4 cup fresh mint leaves
1 1/2 cups fresh orange juice
1/2 cup fresh lemon juice
1 pasteurized egg white, stiffly beaten
1 cup heavy cream
Green food coloring (optional)

Combine the water and sugar in a saucepan. Bring to a boil, stirring constantly until the sugar is dissolved. Remove from the heat. Add the mint leaves. Let stand, covered, for 30 minutes or longer; strain into a bowl. Stir in the orange juice and lemon juice. Chill, covered, until completely cool. Fold in the egg white, cream and food coloring. Pour into an ice cream freezer. Freeze using the manufacturer's directions. *Makes 1 1/2 quarts.*

Chocolate Canela Fondue

$^1/_2$ cup half-and-half

$^1/_4$ cup (or more) milk

$1^1/_3$ cups (8 ounces) semisweet
   chocolate chips

1 canela stick

$1^1/_4$ cups (or more) confectioners' sugar

$^1/_4$ cup water

2 tablespoons dark corn syrup

2 tablespoons vanilla extract

Dash of salt

The word dessert comes from an old French phrase meaning "to clear the table."

Combine the half-and-half, milk, chocolate chips and canela stick in a saucepan. Cook over medium-low heat for 5 minutes or until smooth, stirring constantly. Discard the canela stick. Add the confectioners' sugar, water, corn syrup, vanilla and salt and mix well. Cook for 8 to 10 minutes, stirring constantly and adding additional confectioners' sugar if too thin or additional milk or water if too thick. Pour into a fondue pot and keep warm. Serve with vanilla wafers, marshmallows, pound cake squares, brownies, apple slices, banana slices and/or dried apricots. **Serves 8.**

Southern Peanut Brittle

2/3 cup light corn syrup
1 1/2 cups sugar
2 cups raw peanuts (preferably Spanish peanuts)
Dash of salt
1 teaspoon baking soda

Combine the corn syrup, sugar, peanuts and salt in a medium saucepan and mix well. Cook over medium heat for 15 to 20 minutes or until the peanuts begin to pop or brown. Remove from the heat. Add the baking soda and stir until glossy. Pour onto a greased baking sheet and cool until firm. Break into pieces to serve. **Serves 10.**

White Chocolate—Covered Cranberries

1 package cranberries
1 package white almond bark

Rinse and sort the cranberries. Drain and pat dry with paper towels. Melt the almond bark in a double boiler. Dip the cranberries partially in the melted almond bark, using a wooden pick to hold the cranberries. Place the cranberries on waxed paper to cool. Remove the wooden picks before serving. **Serves 50.**

Cranberry White Chocolate Cheesecake

CRUST

1¹/4 cups graham cracker crumbs

¹/2 cup finely chopped pecans

¹/4 cup packed brown sugar

¹/4 cup granulated sugar

¹/4 cup (¹/2 stick) butter, melted

FILLING

12 ounces white chocolate

¹/2 cup heavy cream

24 ounces cream cheese, softened

1¹/2 cups sugar

5 eggs

2 teaspoons vanilla extract

1¹/2 cups cranberries

To soften brown sugar, place it in a microwave-safe dish with a piece of apple or bread and microwave on High for thirty seconds.

FOR THE CRUST, combine the graham cracker crumbs, pecans, brown sugar, granulated sugar and butter in a bowl and mix well. Press over the bottom of a springform pan. Bake at 325 degrees for 15 minutes.

FOR THE FILLING, combine the white chocolate and cream in a double boiler and cook until the white chocolate is melted, stirring constantly. Let stand until cool. Combine the cream cheese and sugar in a mixing bowl and beat until smooth. Beat in the eggs 1 at a time. Stir in the vanilla. Add the white chocolate mixture and mix well. Stir in the cranberries. Pour into the prepared crust. Bake at 350 degrees for 1 hour or until the center is set.

Serves 20 to 25.

Famous Cheesecake

CRUST

1 cup graham cracker crumbs

1/3 cup ultrafine sugar

1/2 cup flaked coconut

1/2 cup pecan pieces, toasted

1/2 cup (1 stick) butter, melted

TOPPING

2 cups sour cream

1/3 cup ultrafine sugar

1 teaspoon vanilla extract

FILLING

24 ounces cream cheese, softened

1 cup ultrafine sugar

3 eggs

2 teaspoons vanilla extract

FOR THE CRUST, combine the graham cracker crumbs, sugar, coconut and pecans in a bowl and mix well. Add the butter and mix well. Press over the bottom and up the side of a 9- or 12-inch springform pan.

FOR THE TOPPING, combine the sour cream, sugar and vanilla in a bowl and mix well.

FOR THE FILLING, combine the cream cheese and sugar in a mixing bowl and beat until creamy, scraping the side of the bowl frequently. Beat in the eggs 1 at a time. Stir in the vanilla.

Pour the filling into the prepared crust. Bake at 350 degrees for 30 to 45 minutes. Spread with the topping. Bake for 10 minutes. Let stand until cool. Chill, covered, for 12 hours or longer. Remove the side of the pan. Cut the chilled cheesecake into slices. Serve cold or at room temperature. You may serve the cheesecake with fresh fruit or chocolate sauce. *Serves 12 or more.*

Key Lime Cheesecake

2 cups graham cracker crumbs

$1/4$ cup sugar

$1/2$ cup (1 stick) butter, melted

24 ounces cream cheese, softened

$1^1/4$ cups sugar

3 eggs

1 cup sour cream

$1^1/2$ teaspoons grated lime zest

$1/2$ cup Key lime juice

Combine the graham cracker crumbs, $1/4$ cup sugar and the butter in a bowl and mix well. Press over the bottom and 1 inch up the side of a greased 9-inch springform pan. Bake at 350 degrees for 8 minutes. Let stand until cool.

Beat the cream cheese in a mixing bowl until fluffy. Add $1^1/4$ cups sugar gradually, beating constantly. Beat in the eggs 1 at a time. Stir in the sour cream, lime zest and Key lime juice. Pour into the prepared crust. Bake at 325 degrees for 65 minutes.

Turn off the oven and prop the door open. Let the cheesecake stand in the oven for 15 minutes. Run a knife around the edge of the pan and remove the side. Let stand on a wire rack until completely cool. Chill, covered, for 8 hours. Garnish with strawberry halves. *Serves 12 to 14.*

The wine industry in Texas has bottled more than one and one-half million gallons of wine.

Tres Leches Cake

1 cup all-purpose flour
2 teaspoons baking powder
3 egg whites, at room temperature
1 cup sugar
3 egg yolks, at room temperature
$^1/_4$ cup milk
1 cup heavy cream
1 (14-ounce) can sweetened condensed milk
1 (12-ounce) can evaporated milk
$^2/_3$ cup light corn syrup
2 egg whites, at room temperature
1 small package frozen strawberries, thawed (optional)
$^1/_4$ cup sugar (optional)

Combine the flour and baking powder and mix well. Beat 3 egg whites at medium speed in a mixing bowl for 2 to 3 minutes or until soft peaks form. Add 1 cup sugar gradually, beating constantly at high speed. Beat until glossy. Beat in the egg yolks 1 at a time. Add the flour mixture $^1/_4$ at a time, beating constantly. Add the milk and stir until smooth. Pour into a buttered 9×13-inch baking dish. Bake at 325 degrees for 25 to 30 minutes or until the cake tests done. Let stand to cool. Prick the cake at 1-inch intervals using a wooden pick. Combine the cream, sweetened condensed milk and evaporated milk in a bowl and mix well. Pour evenly over the cake. Chill, covered, for 1 hour or longer. Combine the corn syrup and 2 egg whites in a heatproof bowl. Place in a skillet of simmering water. Cook to 140 degrees on a candy thermometer, beating constantly at low speed. Beat for 4 to 5 minutes or until stiff glossy peaks form. Remove the meringue from the heat. Beat for 2 to 3 minutes or until cool. Spread over the cake. Combine the strawberries and $^1/_4$ cup sugar in a blender and process until puréed. Drizzle over the meringue. **Serves 24.**

Pumpkin Bundt Cake

CAKE
1 (2-layer) package yellow cake mix

$1/2$ cup vegetable oil

1 (15-ounce) can pumpkin

$3/4$ cup sugar

$1/4$ cup water

4 eggs

$1^1/2$ teaspoons ground cinnamon

$1/4$ teaspoon nutmeg

CREAM CHEESE FROSTING
3 ounces cream cheese, softened

$1/4$ cup ($1/2$ stick) butter, softened

$1/2$ teaspoon vanilla extract

2 cups sifted confectioners' sugar

FOR THE CAKE, combine the cake mix, oil, pumpkin, sugar, water, eggs, cinnamon and nutmeg in a mixing bowl and beat at medium speed for 2 minutes. Pour into a greased bundt pan. Bake at 350 degrees for 50 to 60 minutes. Let stand until cool. Invert onto a cake plate.

FOR THE FROSTING, combine the cream cheese and butter in a mixing bowl and beat until smooth. Add the vanilla and confectioners' sugar gradually, beating constantly. Beat until light and fluffy.

Spread the frosting over the cooled cake. *Serves 14 to 16.*

Strawberry Cream Cake Roll

When a recipe calls for heavy cream that is to be whipped, vanilla ice cream may be used as a substitute. Place a scoop of ice cream in a stand mixer or hand mixer, let thaw for a couple of minutes, and whip.

CAKE

4 eggs
1 teaspoon vanilla extract
3/4 cup sugar
3/4 cup sifted cake flour
1 teaspoon baking powder
1/4 teaspoon salt
Confectioners' sugar for sprinkling

CREAM FILLING

1 cup heavy whipping cream
1/4 cup sugar
1/2 teaspoon vanilla extract
2 cups sliced strawberries

FOR THE CAKE, combine the eggs and vanilla in a mixing bowl and beat at high speed for 5 minutes or until pale yellow. Add the sugar gradually, beating constantly. Beat until dissolved. Combine the flour, baking powder and salt and mix well. Fold into the egg mixture. Pour into a greased and waxed paper-lined jelly roll pan, spreading evenly. Bake at 375 degrees for 10 to 12 minutes or until light brown. Sprinkle a clean kitchen towel generously with confectioners' sugar. Invert the cake onto the towel. Remove the waxed paper and trim the edges of the cake. Roll the warm cake in the towel as for a jelly roll from 1 short side and place on a wire rack to cool.

FOR THE FILLING, combine the cream, sugar and vanilla in a mixing bowl and beat until stiff peaks form.

Unroll the cooled cake carefully and remove the towel. Spread the cream filling over the cake. Sprinkle with the strawberries and reroll. Wrap in plastic wrap and chill for 2 hours. Garnish with additional strawberries, confectioners' sugar and whipped cream. **Serves 10.**

Milk Chocolate Bar Cake

1 (2-layer) chocolate cake mix
8 ounces cream cheese, softened
1 cup confectioners' sugar
$1/2$ cup granulated sugar
10 milk chocolate bars with almonds, finely chopped
12 ounces whipped topping

Prepare the cake batter using the cake mix package directions. Pour into 3 greased and floured 8-inch cake pans. Bake at 325 degrees for 20 to 25 minutes or until the layers test done. Cool in the pans on wire racks for 10 minutes. Remove the layers to wire racks. Let stand until completely cool. Beat the cream cheese, confectioners' sugar and granulated sugar in a mixing bowl until creamy. Fold in the candy and whipped topping. Spread between the layers and over the top and side of the cooled cake. **Serves 12.**

Million Dollar Pound Cake

2 cups (4 sticks) butter, softened
3 cups sugar
6 eggs
4 cups all-purpose flour
$3/4$ cup milk
1 teaspoon almond extract
1 teaspoon vanilla extract

Combine the butter and sugar in a mixing bowl and beat until creamy. Beat in the eggs 1 at a time. Add the flour alternately with the milk, beating constantly. Stir in the almond extract and vanilla extract. Pour into a greased and floured 10-inch tube pan. Bake at 300 degrees for 1 hour and 40 minutes or until the cake tests done. Cool in the pan for 15 minutes. Remove to a wire rack to cool completely. **Serves 12 to 16.**

White Chocolate Pound Cake

White chocolate is not true chocolate because it contains no chocolate liquor and very little chocolate flavor. It is usually a mix of cocoa butter, sugar, milk solids, lecithin, and vanilla.

8 ounces white chocolate
1 cup (2 sticks) butter, softened
2 cups sugar
5 eggs
2 teaspoons vanilla extract
3 cups all-purpose flour
1 teaspoon baking powder
$^1/_2$ teaspoon salt
$^1/_4$ teaspoon baking soda
1 cup sour cream
2 tablespoons sugar
Melted white chocolate for drizzling (optional)
Melted dark chocolate for drizzling (optional)

Melt 4 ounces of the white chocolate in a double boiler. Chop the remaining 4 ounces white chocolate. Combine the butter and 2 cups sugar in a mixing bowl and beat for 5 minutes. Beat in the eggs 1 at a time. Stir in the vanilla. Add the 4 ounces melted white chocolate and mix well.

Combine the flour, baking powder, salt and baking soda and mix well. Add the flour mixture to the butter mixture alternately with the sour cream, beating constantly.

Sprinkle 2 tablespoons sugar over the bottom of a greased bundt pan. Pour $^1/_3$ of the batter into the prepared pan. Sprinkle with the chopped white chocolate. Add the remaining batter. Bake at 350 degrees for 55 to 60 minutes. Let stand to cool in the pan for 10 minutes. Invert onto a cake plate. Drizzle with melted white chocolate and dark chocolate. **Serves 8.**

Buttermilk Chess Pie

2 cups sugar
1/2 cup (1 stick) butter or
    margarine
3 tablespoons all-purpose flour

3 eggs, beaten
1 cup buttermilk
1 teaspoon vanilla extract
1 unbaked (9-inch) pie shell

Combine the sugar, butter and flour in a mixing bowl and beat until creamy. Beat in the eggs. Add the buttermilk and vanilla and mix well. Pour into the pie shell. Bake at 350 degrees for 45 to 50 minutes. **Serves 6.**

Bourbon Chocolate Pie

1 cup sugar
2 eggs
1/4 cup cornstarch
1/2 cup (1 stick) butter, melted
3 tablespoons bourbon
1 cup (6 ounces) semisweet
    chocolate chips

1 cup pecan halves, chopped
1 unbaked (9-inch) pie shell
1 cup heavy whipping cream
2 tablespoons confectioners'
    sugar
1/2 teaspoon bourbon

Combine the sugar, eggs, cornstarch, butter and 3 tablespoons bourbon in a bowl and mix well. Stir in the chocolate chips and pecans. Pour into the pie shell. Bake at 350 degrees for 30 to 35 minutes or until puffed and brown. Let stand until completely cool. Beat the cream with the confectioners' sugar and 1/2 teaspoon bourbon in a mixing bowl until stiff peaks form. Top each serving of pie with some of the whipped cream mixture. **Serves 6 to 8.**

The word chocolate comes from the Aztec xocolatl, which means "bitter water." Chocolate comes from the tropical cocoa bean. The beans are removed from the pods, dried, fermented, roasted, and cracked to separate them from the shells.

Caramel Coconut Pie

$^1/4$ cup butter or margarine
1 (7-ounce) package flaked coconut
$^1/2$ cup chopped pecans
16 ounces cream cheese, softened
1 (14-ounce) can sweetened condensed milk
16 ounces whipped topping
2 baked piecrusts or vanilla wafer pie shells
1 (12-ounce) jar caramel ice cream topping

Melt the butter in a skillet. Stir in the coconut and pecans. Cook until golden brown, stirring constantly. Combine the cream cheese and sweetened condensed milk in a mixing bowl and beat at medium speed until smooth. Fold in the whipped topping. Pour $^1/4$ of the cream cheese mixture into each piecrust. Drizzle each with $^1/4$ of the ice cream topping and sprinkle with $^1/4$ of the coconut mixture. Layer each with $^1/2$ of the remaining cream cheese mixture, ice cream topping and coconut mixture. Freeze, covered, for 8 hours. Let stand for 5 minutes before slicing. *Serves 16.*

Lemon Icebox Pie

1 cup chocolate wafer crumbs
2 tablespoons sugar
3 tablespoons butter, melted
2 egg yolks, beaten
1 cup sweetened condensed milk
1 tablespoon grated lemon zest
$1/2$ cup fresh lemon juice
$1/2$ teaspoon almond extract
2 egg whites
$1/4$ cup sugar

Combine the chocolate wafer crumbs, 2 tablespoons sugar and the butter in a bowl and mix well. Reserve 2 tablespoons of the crumb mixture. Press the remaining crumb mixture over the bottom of a pie plate. Chill, covered, until firm. Combine the egg yolks, sweetened condensed milk, lemon zest, lemon juice and almond extract in a saucepan and mix well. Cook over low heat until thickened, stirring constantly. Let stand until cool. Beat the egg whites in a mixing bowl until foamy. Add $1/4$ cup sugar gradually, beating constantly. Beat until stiff peaks form. Fold into the cooled lemon mixture. Pour into the prepared pie plate. Sprinkle with the reserved crumb mixture. Freeze, covered, for 3 hours or longer. Remove from the freezer 5 minutes before serving time. You may make this pie in a 9×9-inch pan. *Serves 6 to 8.*

Apricot Macaroons

3 ounces dried apricots (about $1/2$ cup packed)
$1/2$ cup water
$3/4$ cup plus 1 tablespoon sugar
3 egg whites
$4^1/2$ cups unsweetened shredded coconut

Cut each apricot into 3 or 4 pieces. Combine the apricots, water and
1 tablespoon of the sugar in a saucepan. Cook over medium heat until the
apricots are tender. Let stand to cool slightly.

Combine the apricot mixture, remaining $3/4$ cup sugar, the egg whites and
$1/2$ cup of the coconut in a food processor and pulse until the apricots are
puréed. Pour into a bowl. Add the remaining coconut and stir until the
mixture holds together. Shape into 24 balls. Arrange on a parchment-lined
cookie sheet.

Bake at 350 degrees for 15 to 20 minutes or until light brown. Cool on
the cookie sheet for 2 minutes. Remove to a wire rack to cool completely.
Store in an airtight container. **Makes 2 dozen cookies.**

*Sugar is a natural
carbohydrate made through
photosynthesis, usually from
either sugarcane or sugar
beets. Its chemical name
is sucrose.*

Gingerbread Men

1/3 cup shortening
1 cup packed brown sugar
1 1/2 cups molasses
1 1/2 cups cold water
6 cups sifted all-purpose flour
1 teaspoon salt
1 teaspoon ground ginger
1 teaspoon ground allspice
1 teaspoon ground cloves
2 teaspoons ground cinnamon
2 teaspoons baking soda
3 tablespoons cold water
1 cup (about) sifted all-purpose flour

Combine the shortening, brown sugar and molasses in a bowl and mix well. Add 1 1/2 cups cold water and mix well. Sift 6 cups flour, the salt, ginger, allspice, cloves and cinnamon into a bowl. Add the baking soda and 3 tablespoons cold water and mix well. Add the shortening mixture and mix well. Mix in enough of 1 cup flour to make a stiff dough. Refrigerate, covered, until chilled. Roll 1/4 inch thick on a lightly floured surface. Cut with a gingerbread man cookie cutter. Decorate as desired with red hot cinnamon candies, raisins and so forth. Remove to a lightly greased cookie sheet using a wide spatula. Bake at 350 degrees for 12 to 15 minutes. **Makes 30 cookies.**

Chocolate Chip Oatmeal Cookies

Shape the cookie dough into balls, place on cookie sheets, and freeze. Place in freezer bags and freeze until ready to bake. Arrange the balls on a cookie sheet and bake at 200 degrees for 10 minutes to thaw. Bake at 350 degrees for 10 to 12 minutes or until light golden brown.

1 cup shortening
3/4 cup packed brown sugar
3/4 cup granulated sugar
2 eggs
1 teaspoon hot water
1 to 2 teaspoons vanilla extract
1 1/2 cups all-purpose flour
1 teaspoon baking soda
1 teaspoon salt
1 cup chopped pecans
2 cups rolled oats
1 1/3 cups (8 ounces) semisweet chocolate chips

Combine the shortening, brown sugar and granulated sugar in a mixing bowl and beat until creamy. Beat in the eggs. Add the hot water and vanilla and mix well. Sift the flour, baking soda and salt together. Add to the shortening mixture and mix well. Fold in the pecans, oats and chocolate chips. Drop by heaping teaspoonfuls onto a nonstick cookie sheet. Bake at 350 degrees for 10 to 12 minutes or until light golden brown. **Makes 6 dozen cookies.**

Ranger Cookies

1 cup shortening
1 cup granulated sugar
1 cup packed brown sugar
2 eggs
1 teaspoon vanilla extract
2 cups all-purpose flour
1 teaspoon salt
1 teaspoon baking soda
$1/2$ teaspoon baking powder
1 cup rolled oats
2 cups crisp rice cereal
1 cup flaked coconut
1 cup chopped nuts

There are many varieties of sugar to choose from, depending on the type of dish being baked. Besides the size of the granules (granulated, pearl, superfine, and powdered), there are also varieties of darkness: light brown, golden, dark brown, muscovado (light and dark), and turbinado (raw sugar).

Combine the shortening, granulated sugar and brown sugar in a mixing bowl and beat until creamy. Beat in the eggs and vanilla. Sift the flour, salt, baking soda and baking powder together. Add to the shortening mixture and mix well. Fold in the oats, cereal, coconut and nuts. Drop by teaspoonfuls onto a nonstick cookie sheet. Bake at 350 degrees for 10 to 12 minutes.
Makes 5 dozen cookies.

Raspberry Almond Shortbread Thumbprints

2/3 cup sugar
1 cup (2 sticks) butter, softened
1/2 teaspoon almond extract
2 cups all-purpose flour
1/2 cup raspberry jam
1 cup confectioners' sugar
1 1/2 teaspoons almond extract
2 to 4 teaspoons water

Combine the sugar, butter and 1/2 teaspoon almond extract in a mixing bowl and beat at medium speed until creamy. Add the flour gradually, beating constantly at low speed. Beat until well mixed. Shape into 1-inch balls. Arrange 2 inches apart on a nonstick cookie sheet. Make an indentation in each cookie using your thumb; edges may crack slightly. Fill each indentation with about 1/4 teaspoon jam. Bake at 350 degrees until light brown. Cool on the cookie sheet for 1 minute. Remove to a wire rack to cool completely. Combine the confectioners' sugar and 1 1/2 teaspoons almond extract in a bowl and mix well. Stir in enough of the water to make a thin glaze. Drizzle over the cookies in a crosshatch pattern.
Makes 3 1/2 dozen cookies.

Snickerdoodles

$2^2/3$ cups all-purpose flour
1 cup (2 sticks) butter or margarine, softened
2 teaspoons cream of tartar
1 teaspoon baking soda
$1/2$ teaspoon salt
$1/2$ teaspoon vanilla extract
2 eggs
$1^1/2$ cups sugar
2 teaspoons cinnamon

Combine the flour, butter, cream of tartar, baking soda, salt, vanilla, eggs and $1^1/4$ cups of the sugar in a mixing bowl. Beat at low speed until well blended, scraping the bowl occasionally using a rubber spatula. Shape into a ball and wrap in plastic wrap. Refrigerate for 8 to 10 hours or until easy to handle. Combine the cinnamon and the remaining $1/4$ cup sugar in a bowl and mix well. Shape the dough into balls using a $1^1/2$-inch scoop. Coat with the cinnamon-sugar and arrange 2 inches apart on an ungreased cookie sheet. Bake at 400 degrees for 10 minutes or until light brown. Remove to a wire rack to cool. Store in an airtight container. ***Makes (about) 5 dozen cookies.***

There are many varieties of sugar available, depending on the type of dish being baked. Besides the sizes of the granules (granulated, pearl, superfine and powdered), there are also varieties of darkness: light brown, golden, dark brown, muscovado (light and dark) and turbinado (raw sugar).

Coffee Lovers' Brownies

BROWNIES

2 tablespoons instant coffee
 granules
1 tablespoon boiling water
8 ounces bittersweet chocolate
3/4 cup (1 1/2 sticks) butter
1 1/2 cups sugar
2 teaspoons vanilla extract
4 eggs
1 cup all-purpose flour
1/2 teaspoon salt
1 cup finely chopped pecans

FROSTING

6 tablespoons butter, softened
8 ounces cream cheese, softened
1 1/2 cups confectioners' sugar
1 teaspoon vanilla extract
1 teaspoon ground cinnamon

GLAZE

1 1/2 teaspoons instant coffee
 granules
1 tablespoon boiling water
6 ounces bittersweet chocolate
2 tablespoons butter
2 tablespoons heavy cream

FOR THE BROWNIES, dissolve the coffee granules in the boiling water in a bowl. Cook the chocolate and butter in a double boiler until melted, stirring constantly. Remove from the heat. Stir in the coffee mixture until smooth. Let stand until lukewarm. Stir in the sugar and vanilla. Beat in the eggs 1 at a time. Add the flour and salt and stir just until mixed. Stir in the pecans. Spread evenly in a greased 9×13-inch baking pan. Bake at 350 degrees for 20 to 25 minutes; the center should still be moist. Let stand until completely cool.

FOR THE FROSTING, combine the butter and cream cheese in a mixing bowl and beat until creamy. Add the confectioners' sugar, vanilla and cinnamon and mix well. Chill, covered, until set. Spread over the cooled brownies; chill.

FOR THE GLAZE, dissolve the coffee granules in the boiling water in a bowl. Combine the coffee mixture, chocolate, butter and cream in a saucepan and cook over low heat, stirring constantly until smooth. Spread carefully over the chilled frosted brownies. Chill, covered, for 3 hours or longer before cutting into squares. Serve chilled or at room temperature.
Makes 2 dozen brownies.

Cookbook Committee

Chairman
Kathy Rollo

Assistant Chairman
Gwen Belk

Art and Design
Charly Johnson

Recipes
Susan McDonald

Non-Recipe Text
Susan Vasquez

Marketing
Simone Barnhill

Sustaining Advisors
Phyllis Jones and Stephanie McKee

Past President
Cray Pickering

President
Lori Rice-Spearman

President-Elect
Deborah Finlayson

Contributors

John D. Adams
Sharon Adams
Sandy Adling
Barbara Airhart
Linda Alderson
Debbie Allen
Sarah Ancell
Shelby Anderson
Frances Ansley
Wendy Armes
Louise Arnold
Gay Atkins
Bonnie Aycock
Tracy Bacon
Gayle Bailey
Simone Barnhill
Lisa Bartee
Carol Jean Bartlett
Stacy Bates
Gwen McDill Belk
Clarissa Bell
Laura Nichole Bennett
Kim Bevers
Jan Blackwell
Elise Blodgett
Connie Sterling Blosser
Mackie Bobo
Kellye Bouldin
Kasi Boutwell
Connie Bowers
Kristy Boyd
Jan Adair Bradley
Ruth Anne Brazill
Ronda Brewer
Kathy Britton
Matt Britton
Lacy Greenstreet Brown
Mary Burke
Terri Byrne
Lynn Calloway
Alana Carr
Jon Ann Carter

Deena Caskey
Colleen Cauley
Donna Chandler
Kelli Childre
Cherry Clark
Jan Combest
Christy Condra
Robin Conkwright
Sandy Core
Karen Courtney
Marilyn Crawford
Margie Croft
Ann Cruce-Roberts
Heather Cummings
Alice Ann Cunningham
Gayle Cunningham
Becky Davis
Brandy Davis
Debi Davis
Johnnie Sue Dayton
Mellessa Denny
Stacey Derr
Kelly DeSplinter
Debbie deTournillon
Cari Dillon
Becky Drachenberg
Sharon Dykes
Nancy Eagan
Diane Earl
Janis L. Elam-Blackwell
Deborah Finlayson
Jone Fisher
Lynn Forbess
Yvette Foshee
Dawne Franks
Julie Freund
Glory Fuller
Beth Furgerson
Katie Gamueda
Christy Genenbacher
Louise Gilkerson
Janeen Holmes Gilliam

Robin Going
Linda Greenstreet
Mindy Griffin
Rose Jean Griffith
Cindy Guinn
Amy Hanson
Carolyn Harding
Tommie Hatch
Kay Hatton
Sandra Hester
Ami E. Hill-Rendon
Heather Hocker
Mary Frances Holly
Terry Hood
Cynthia Howard
Kay Howard
Sheree Huddleston
Fay Dean Huneke
Stacey Janczak
Ali Johnson
Ann Johnson
Charly Johnson
Judy Johnson
Ann Johnston
Jana Johnston
Paula Joiner
Betsy Goebel Jones
Phyllis J. Jones
Virginia Joplin
Pat Jordan
Toni Jordan
Latrelle Bright Joy
Marjorie C. Kastman
Cayce Kaufman
Karen Kay
Cheryl Keefer
Carolyn Kennedy
Shannon Kirkland
Celia Kuykendall
Melissa Kuykendall
Kendra Lansdell
Merrill Laurentz

Ginda Greenstreet Level
Pat Lewis
Liane Locke
Traci Loveless
Patti Lupton
Brandie MacKenzie
Ruth Martin
Susan Martin
Bonnie Mather
Jennifer Mattison
Peggy Mayes
Amy Maynard
Lynn McClendon
Cindy McCuistion
M'Lee McDonald
Susan Raines McDonald
Stephanie McKee
Karen McMahon
Connie Gatlin McMillian
Lucile McNeal
Angela Medlock
Michelle Melcher
Kathy Miller
Linda Miller
Charlotte L. Moody
Linda L. Moore
Gena Morris
Helen Morris
Leslie Moss
Sheri Mudd
Carolyn Neal
Sandy Ogletree
Melissa Olson
Loretta Owen
Judy Parker
Jean Pasewark
Jeannie Patterson
Melinda Paxton
Sondra Perez
Sandra Peterson
Bebe Petree
Kay Phelps

Nancy Henry Phillips
Cray Pickering
Cathy Spoonts Porter
Cindy Pratas
Melanie Ragain
Taunya Crawford
    Randolph
Dana Reeger
Cathleen Reid
Sandra Reynolds
Kristie Richards
Thresa Rieff
Carol Robertson
Lillian Robertson
Kelly Rodgers
Kathy Rollo
Judy Jay Rostad
Debbie Rubin
Kimberly Rutledge
Linda Sadler
Kay Salem
Jeni Sanders
Kaci Scott
Sharon Shavor
Jenny Shaw
Jennifer Shipman
Robin Sittre
Linsae Snider
Marge Snyder
Nicky Standlee
Amy Stephens
Roni Stiff
Mary Katherine Strong
Tootie Tatum
Joan Taylor
LesLee Laylor
Grady Terrill
Kathy Terrill
Kim Thomas
Marilee Thomas
Celeste Thompson
Tara Thrash

Kay Timberlake
Mandy Tomlin
Jan Tonroy
Page Tumlinson
Paula Tumlinson
Renée Underwood
David Vasquez
Susan Crawford Vasquez
Ann Vaughn
Barbara Vinson
Jenna Vinson
Andrea Wade
Amy Walker
Jo Beth Walker
Betty Wall
Sharla Wallace
Tracey Wallace
Karla Wardroup
Jane Rogers Watt
Kelley Weil
Carole Collier Wesley
Mary Wheat
Pat Wheeler
Helen Wiechmann
Sandra Wiechmann
Holly Wierzba
Sonia Wierzba
Mary Willard
Ann Williams
Laura Crawford Williams
Tammy Williams
Elaine Wilson
Vivian Wilson
Caroline Wylie
Martha York
Mitzi Ziegner
Dawn Zuerker

Index

234

238

A Perfect Setting

The Junior League of Lubbock, Inc.

4205 84th Street
Lubbock, Texas 79423
(806) 794-8874

Name

Address

City   State   Zip

Telephone

Your Order	Qty	Total
A *Perfect Setting* at $27.00 per book		$
Postage and handling at $2.70 per book		$
Total		$

Method of Payment: [ ] MasterCard   [ ] VISA

[ ] Check payable to The Junior League of Lubbock

Account Number   Expiration Date

Signature

Proceeds benefit charitable projects in the Lubbock community.

Photocopies accepted.